SPECTACULAR!

STAGE DESIGN

SendPoints

SPECTACULAR! Stage Design

© SendPoints Publishing Co., Ltd.

SendPoints

EDITED & PUBLISHED BY SendPoints Publishing Co., Ltd.
PUBLISHER: Lin Gengli
PUBLISHING DIRECTOR: Lin Shijian
EDITORIAL DIRECTOR: Sundae Li
EXECUTIVE EDITOR: Christina Hwang, Ye Guangqian
ART DIRECTOR: He Wanling
EXECUTIVE ART EDITOR: Lin Qiumei
PROOFREADING: Sundae Li, Josef Ho

ADDRESS: Room 15A Block 9 Tsui Chuk Garden, Wong Tai Sin, Kowloon, Hong Kong
TEL: +852-35832323 / **FAX:** +852-35832448
EMAIL: info@sendpoints.cn

DISTRIBUTED BY Guangzhou SendPoints Book Co., Ltd.
SALES MANAGER: Zhang Juan (China), Sissi (International)
GUANGZHOU: +86-20-89095121
BEIJING: +86-10-84139071
SHANGHAI: +86-21-63523469
EMAIL: overseas01@sendpoints.cn
WEBSITE: www.sendpoints.cn

ISBN 978-988-13834-8-8

CONCERTS
★ ★ ★
EVENTS & CEREMONIES
★ ★ ★
THEATERS

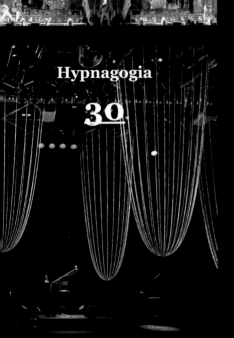

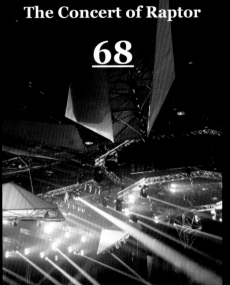

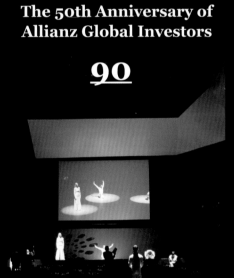
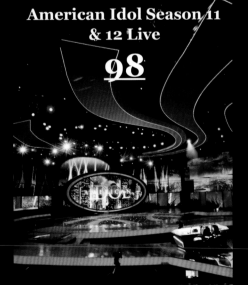

Bethlehem Christmas

108

Home for Christmas

112

The 15th Essence Music Festival

116

The 16th Essence Music Festival

122

H2O Music Festival

130

London 2012 Olympic Closing Ceremony

136

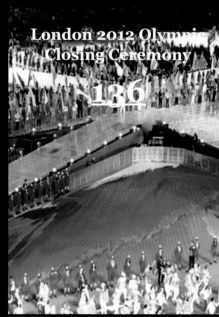

The 11th Myer Spring-Summer Collections Launch

144

The 85th Oscars Academy Awards

148

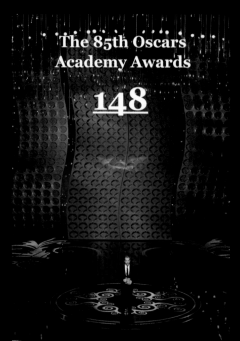

The Voice of Germany

154

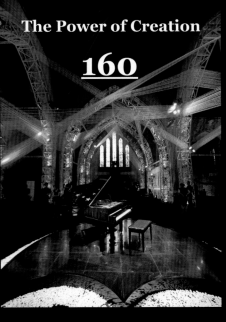
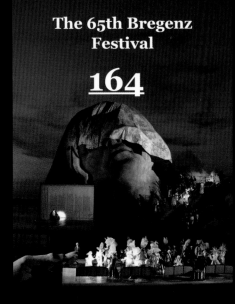
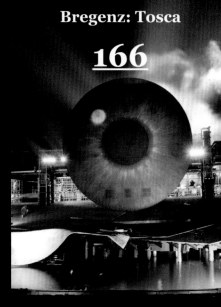

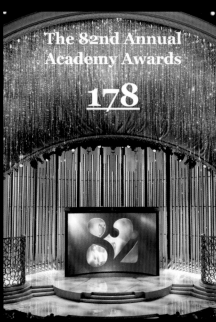

ANTIGONE, ISRAEL

200

Batman Live, World Arena Tour

204

CABARET, ISRAEL

212

DOV GIOVANNI, ISRAEL

עך כך החרדות את חייבת לגבור.

Dispel your grief and fear.

210

Harvey

220

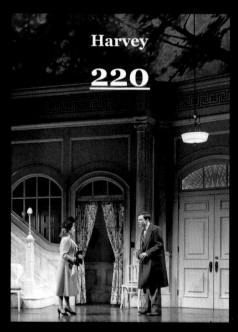

iTMOi

222

Kinky Boots

228

Lucia di Lammermoor

234

The Normal Heart

238

Tartuffe
242

The Master and Margarita
246

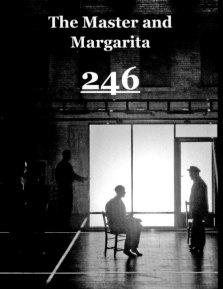

In the Sign of Libra III
250

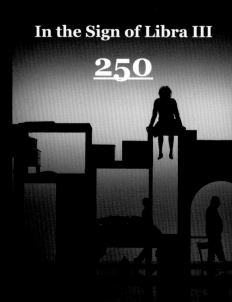

Uncle Vanya
254

Catch Me If You Can
258

Medea & Edipo a Colono Scenography
262

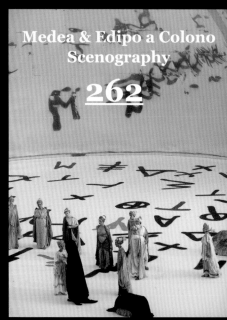

AIDA
266

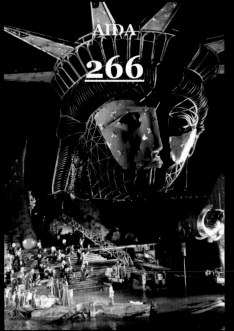

✶✶✶
CONCERTS

Design for concert stages owes its importance to the interaction between the performers and audiences in terms of using and integrating the media technologies. It combines the characteristics of traditional stages with the strength of various technologies, resulting in an effect of harmonious coordination in presenting the ideas of the concert makers, the charm of the performers and the featured information.

New media technologies play an essential role in the stage design for concerts. They are mastered and utilized by designers with high degree of professional proficiency in stage designed for concerts. In this category of stage design, many elements of new media technologies, such as light, shadow, production and air, overlapping, varying and permeation, making the mysterious space of stage with endless and limitless marvellous spectacle.

Progress Stadium Tour

• *The Standing Giant*

Progress Live was performed by British pop group Take That, the eighth of their tours, sponsored by Samsung. As a support to their sixth studio album, in this tour they visited the major cities in UK and the European continent. It was also the first time that the five members performed together since 1995.

Creative Director / Choreographer: Kim Gavin

Production Designer: Es Devlin

Costume Designer: Michael Sharp

Lighting Designer: Patrick Woodroffe

Video Designer: Treatment Studio

This was the second project of Es undertaking with the British band and their Creative Director Kim Gavin, to come up with the concept of a giant man standing up in the center of the stadium independently. They took the project to a number of construction companies, but they were informed that it was impossible to achieve within the available time frame. Ultimately, Brilliant Stages of UK said yes. Then, a great idea of stage design was eventually realized.

· The Design Idea of Progress Tour ·

"We did hundreds of drawings by computer keyboards with all different permutations and variations of a giant man at one end of the stadium, and a giant computer at the other, and a keyboard in the middle. Then we kept coming back to the idea of a breaking dam. That became very important from the lyrics of The Flood", said Devlin.

Progress Live was the eighth concert of Take That's tour, one of the most popular British pop groups. It was the first tour featuring five original members performing together in the last 15 years. The show lasted eight nights continuously at Etihad Stadium in Manchester and Wembley Stadium in London.

With the help of the fantastic stage design, the tour had gained applauses from critics, media and their old and new fans. As one of the greatest designers in England who was the stage designer of London 2012 Olympic Closing Ceremony, Es Devlin, acted as the set designer of this show. She designed a stage dominated by a 30-metre high giant man—OM, which was "holding the show together" literally, in her words.

— The Giant Man "OM"

A two-stage telescopic "spine mast" formed the main component of the structure, providing the giant man OM with support and lift for its sitting and standing positions. The outer section of the mast effectively served as the spine, while two extending inner sections acted as a lifting prop. The whole figure was mounted on a self-propelled mobile base of 1.5m high seated on a 35-ton modified articulated trailer. In show mode, the trailer extended to 12.8m, which stretched OM's legs out in front of itself and contracted to 8.8m to draw its legs up into a crouched position before standing. OM performed the moves including a sweeping motion of the arms, nodding the head, raising each of the singers in the palm of his hands, until eventually moving out in a recumbent position into the middle of the arena. As it did so, it carried the band members on each hand and on platforms set within its abdomen.

— The Idea

All in all, with its acrobats, unicycles and mechanical elephants, the tour with the fantastic design was one of the most lavish ever staged. In Es Devlin's idea, stage designer needs to create a visual world that an audience can believe and trust in. However, the audience would pick up the slightest visual signals, and the designer has to be quick to stay ahead of them.

In 2009, the concept for Progress Live was hatched by the band, plus Devlin and creative director Kim Gavin. They listened and felt the soul of the album "Progress" at a rural inn outside the urban hub of London. Four days later, they had the idea to show man's evolving from ape to astronaut. The electronic feeling of Progress was conveyed on the show by the giant man. Furthermore, "circuit-board lines in the shape of human veins" also had been created featuring sensory elements by Devlin, Gavin and their team.

Aaron Kwok De Showy Masquerade World Tour

• A Transformer Stage

Hong Kong pop singer Aaron Kwok, widely known for his dance skills throughout Asia presented a dance party with his all-new Transformer stage for Aaron Kwok De Showy Masquerade World Tour Live.

Creative Director: Aaron Kwok, Leung May May

Stage Designer: Cheng Yu Kwun, Fion Cheng

Content Designer: dontbelieveinstyle (DBIS)

Lighting Designer: Chow Chung Lung

Executive Producer: Kam Kwong Shing

Show Director: Lam Man On, Jack

Photo Credit: Mic-GO, Zenki@mPowder

Total Area: 20m x 20m

Aaron Kwok De Showy Masquerade World Tour featured a "Transformer" stage that allowed Kwok to sing and dance on it in different parts of the concert. Kwok and stage designers Cheng Yu Kwun and Fion Cheng made use of six trampolines of different sizes suspended in the air, allowing the singer to jump two meters high into the air allowing the singer to jump 2 meters high into the air in breathtaking choreography. The production was a centered stage rather than an end stage. DBIS produced an interactive 3D mapping show for the countdown performance part, as well as a series of stunning undersea graphics to go with the king dancer's amazing steps.

Biffy Clyro Arena
Tour 2013

• "Opposites" Tour + Tree Structure

Biffy Clyro is a trio from Scotland. In its UK arena tour, the trio played 11 shows, in support of their new album Opposites around the country, kicking off at Newcastle Metro Radio Arena 20, expanding to Cardiff, Manchester, Glasgow etc, and finishing up at London O2 Arena.

Creative Director/Art Director: Misty Buckley

Production Company: Paddy Hocken

Client: Biffy Clyro

Production designer Misty Buckley designed a mind blowing stage for Biffy Clyro that drew inspiration from the front cover of the band's new album—a symbol of growth and a twist of a tree. Buckley took a further step on the tree structure and created the internal human body details with skeletons and organs. Buckley revealed the heart and soul of the band with a sculptural representation of Da Vinci's anatomical drawings. The set was like a human structure background and with a huge screen behind, served as an incredible tool to tell stories about the evolution so apparent in the album, the individuals and, ultimately, the show.

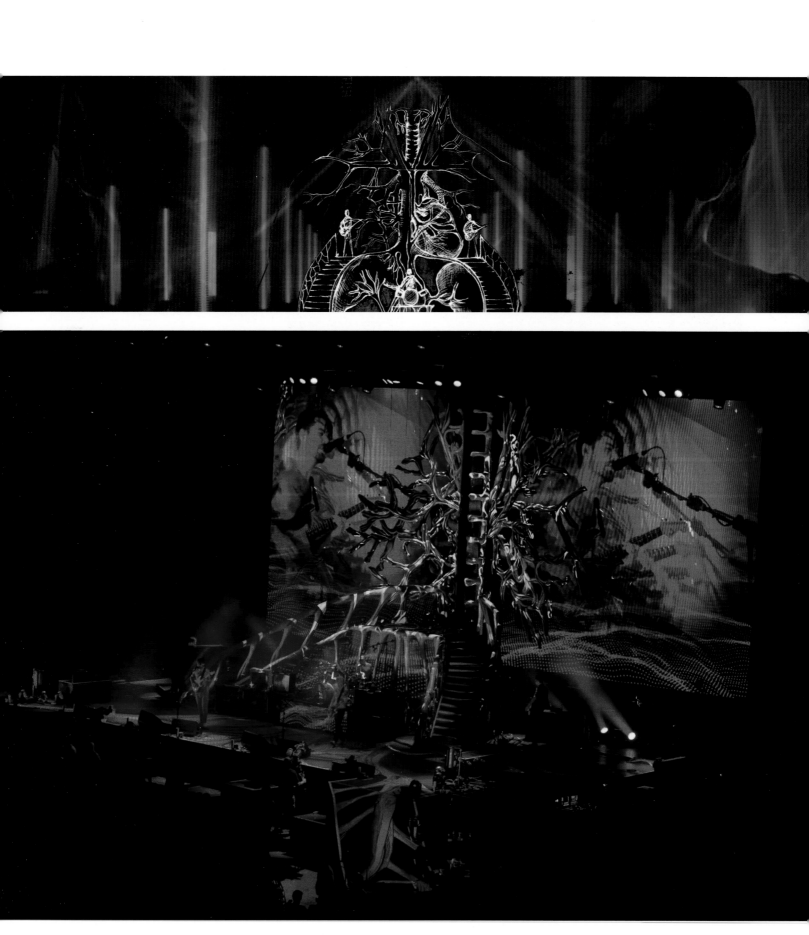

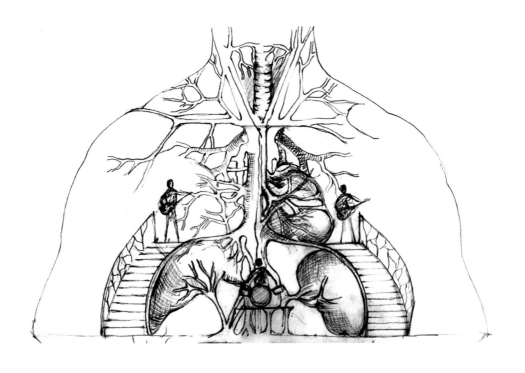

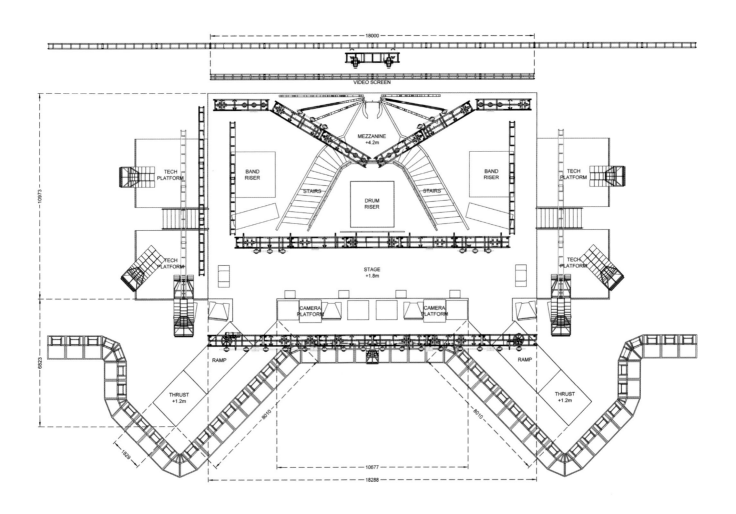

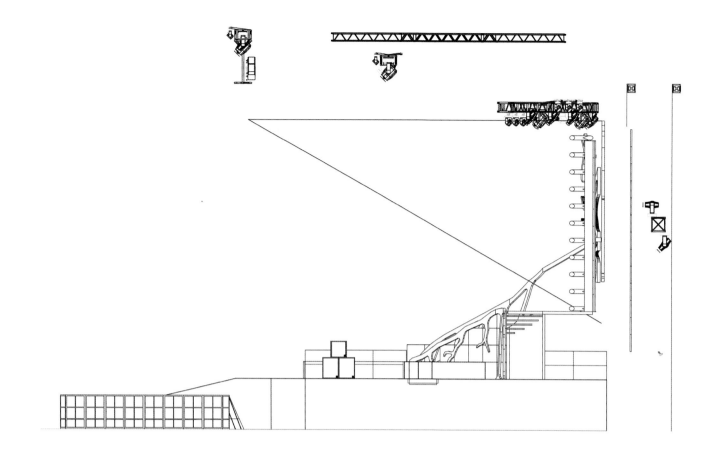

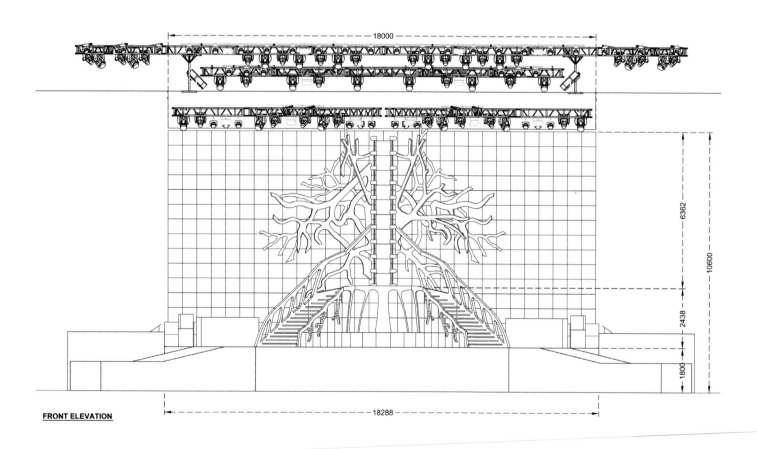

FRONT ELEVATION

Hypnagogia Tokyo

• *Reversed Chain Domes*

Japanese studio Ryo Matsui Architects used steel chains to create the upside-down domes for the stage of a music recital in Tokyo.

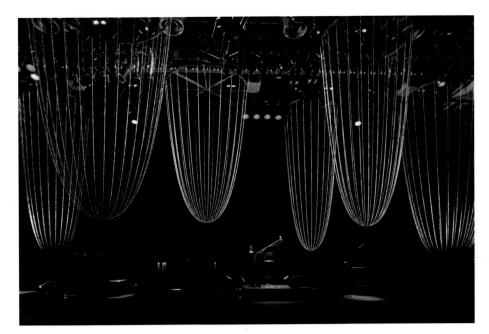

Creative Director: Bun-oh Fujisawa

Designer: Ryo Matsui

Client: M-Site

The domes were created taking full advantage of gravitational law and aggregating 88 catenary curves which were hanging down from a circular structure and gathered towards to the centrosphere. By turning on the light, seven domes present various light and shadow effect, existence of gravity and the feeling of an invisible world rising in the air. It stimulates the audience's five senses throughout the emotional stage-installation. Dramatizing the overall atmosphere, light variations were projected to reflect various musical melodies.

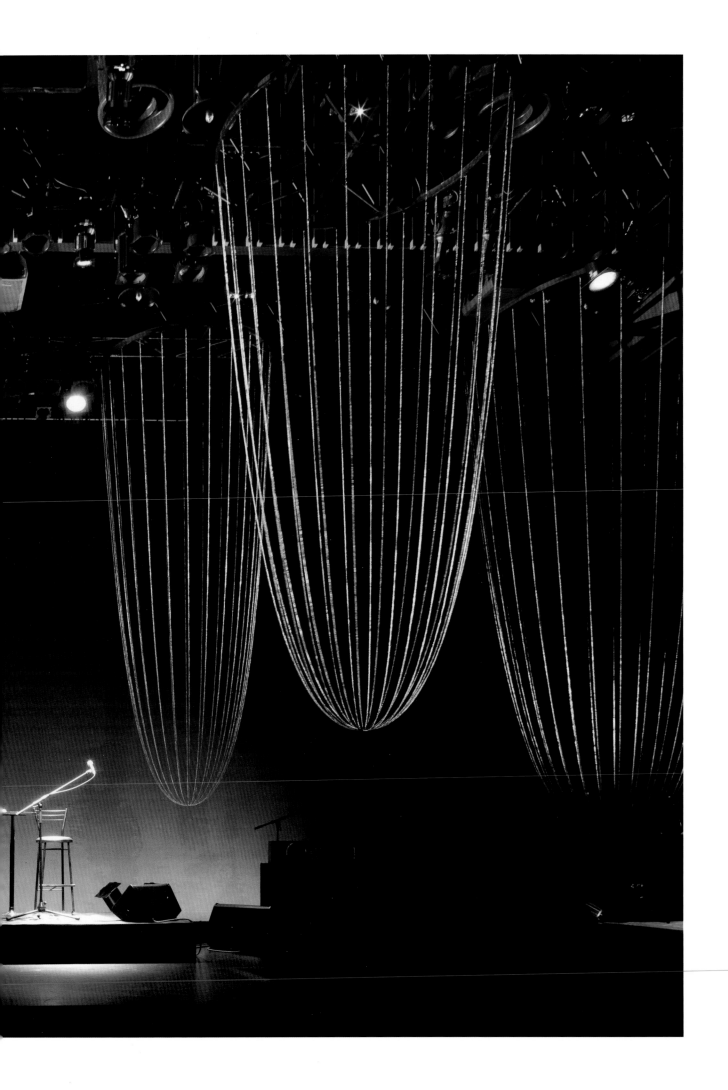

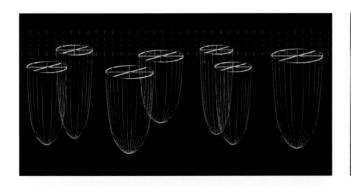

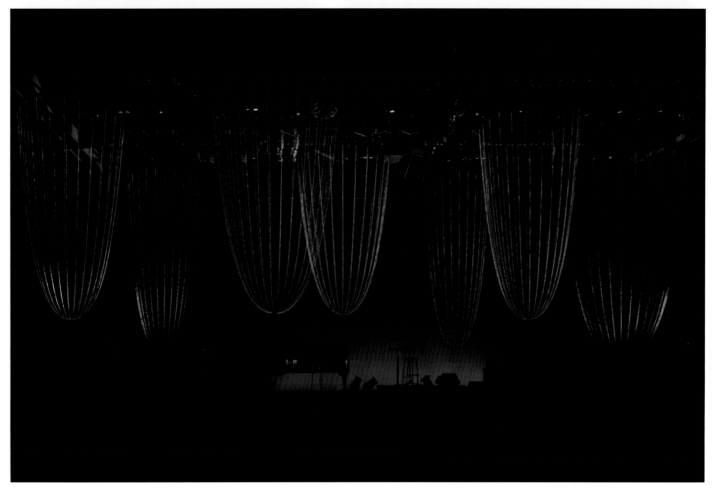

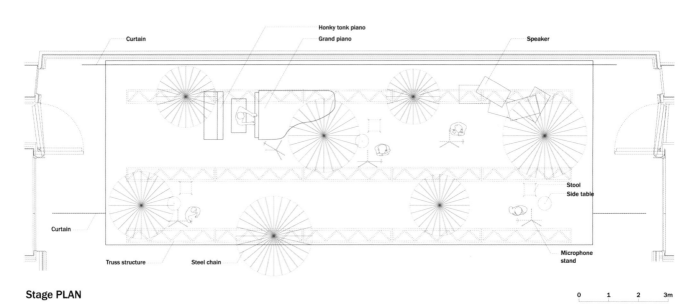

Curtain

Honky tonk piano
Grand piano

Speaker

Stool
Side table

Curtain

Truss structure   Steel chain

Microphone
stand

Stage PLAN

0   1   2   3m

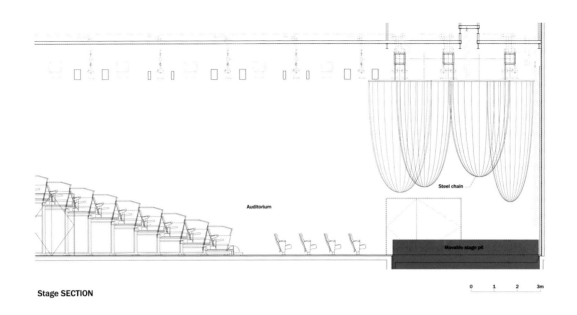

Stage SECTION

Auditorium

Steel chain

Movable stage pit

0   1   2   3m

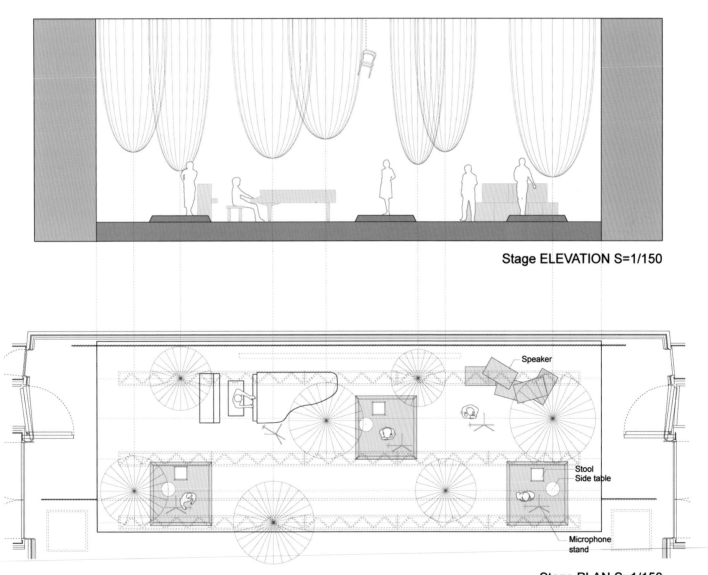

Stage ELEVATION S=1/150

Speaker

Stool
Side table

Microphone
stand

Stage PLAN S=1/150

0   1000   2000   3000

Because We Can Tour

• What About Now Album + Living Kinetic Sculpture

Bon Jovi's 2013 Because We Can World Tour, in support of the band's twelfth album, What About Now, took the band to more than 60 cities across five continents. Named for the album's lead single, the tour was a career milestone that garnered wide acclaim.

Production Designer: Spike Brant (PEDG)

Director of Programming: Felix Peralta (PEDG)

Video Content Designer: Moment Factory

Other Video Content: Meteor Tower

Lighting Designer: Spike Brant (PEDG)

Set Engineering and Production: Tait Towers

Show Control: Control Freak Systems

Photo credit: Moment Factory & David Bergman

Performance Environment Design Group (PEDG) collaborated with Montreal-based new media and entertainment company Moment Factory to bring together a larger-than-life kinetic scenography with stunning visual content. Partnering with scenic technology experts Tait Towers, they developed more than 70 mobile stage elements, including 40 hexagonal towers arranged in a gentle curve behind the stage, and 32 individual lighting winches that moved in synchronicity. Moment Factory created 360° content for the towers, which could be individually reconfigured, raised and lowered, to create different shapes for the projected animations, providing a vast range of backdrop options. The synergy in content and motion produced a living kinetic structure on a spectacular scale.

Control Freak Systems designed the control system and contributed custom software for the Ai Infinity 8 media servers. Supplied by Avolites Media, these servers integrated the movement of the live sculpture with the projected content. Moment Factory and Control Freak Systems worked in tandem with the state of the art system, which allowed greater freedom in programming the show and resulted in a seamless integration of the dynamic content.

WHAT ABOUT NOW

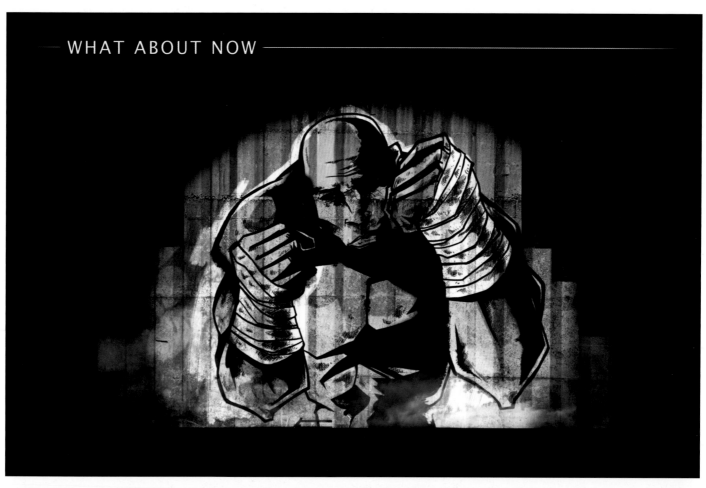

ARMY OF ONE

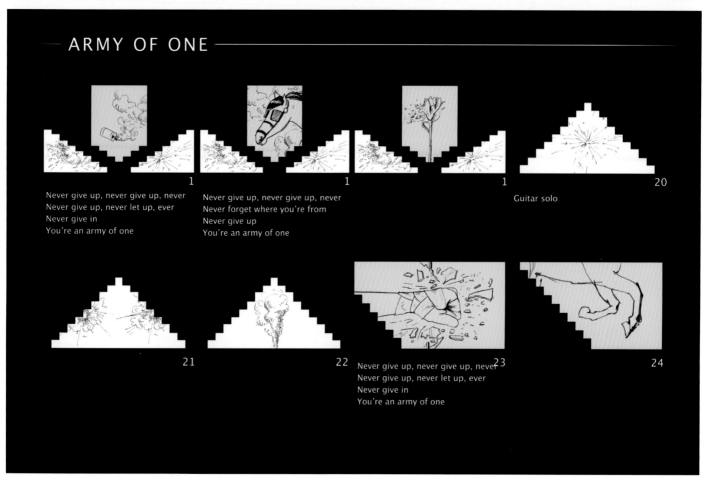

Never give up, never give up, never
Never give up, never let up, ever
Never give in
You're an army of one

Never give up, never give up, never
Never forget where you're from
Never give up
You're an army of one

Guitar solo

1   1   1   20

21   22   23   24

Never give up, never give up, never
Never give up, never let up, ever
Never give in
You're an army of one

WE WEREN'T BORN TO FOLLOW

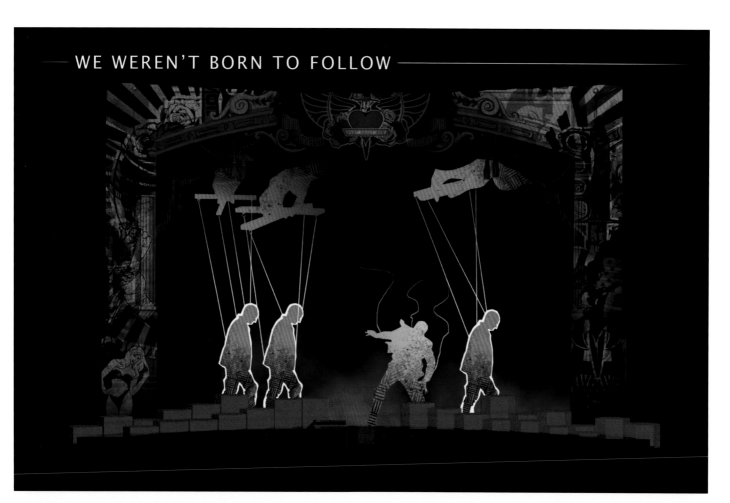

WHAT ABOUT NOW

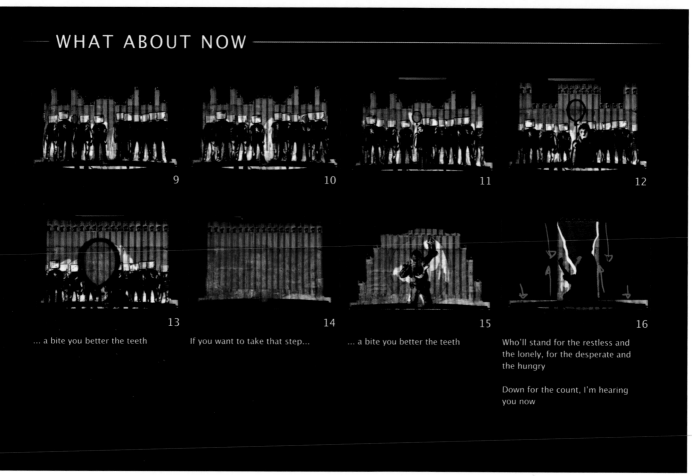

9

10

11

12

13

14

15

16

... a bite you better the teeth

If you want to take that step...

... a bite you better the teeth

Who'll stand for the restless and the lonely, for the desperate and the hungry

Down for the count, I'm hearing you now

How To Destray Angels Tour

• String Screen

The How to Destroy Angels' 2013 Tour stopped in twelve cities across North America, and included a midnight Coachella performance. Inspired and co-created by the band, the innovative and dynamic set took their performances to new heights.

To compliment the innovative and dynamic set designed by long-time Nine Inch Nails production designer Roy Bennett, Moment Factory created a mixture of pre-rendered and real-time visuals. Close collaboration with Trent Reznor and Rob Sheridan (the band's artistic director) was central to the tour's design concept. Strings made of translucent plastic, custom-designed by Bennett, created 3D depth effects and other volumetric lighting tricks. The interactive system, designed by Moment Factory, allowed visual effects to be generated live, providing Sheridan with real-time control of visuals during the show. In combination with the striking stage design, the flexibility of this system opened new avenues of perceptual experimentation.

Creative Director: Rob Sheridan, Trent Reznor

Production Designer: Roy Bennett

Lighting Designer: Roy Bennett

Video Content Designer: Moment Factory, Rob Sheridan

Photo credit: Moment Factory

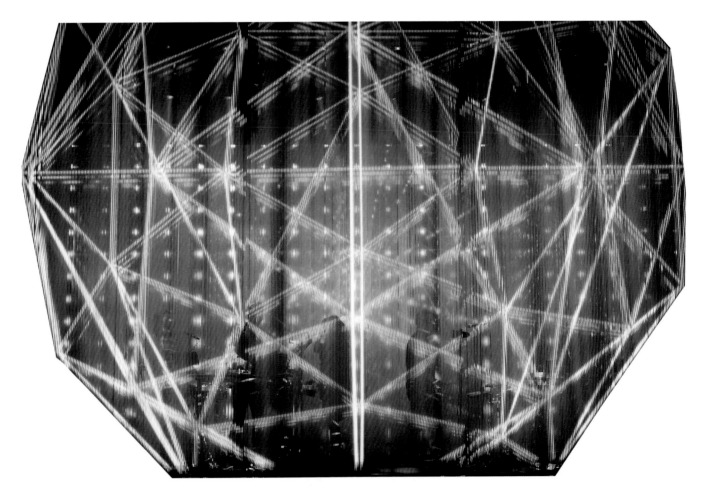

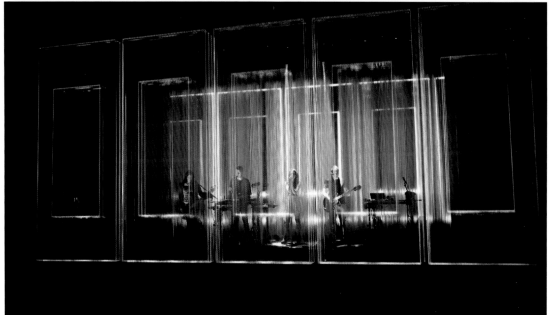

Infected Mushroom Tour

• Futuristic Sculpture

Infected Mushroom is an Israeli duo formed in 1996 in Haifa by producers Erez Eisen and Amit Duvdevani. It has been one of the best-selling groups in Israel's music history. Infected Mushroom's live shows were characterized by vocals and analogue instruments set by multi-media backdrops.

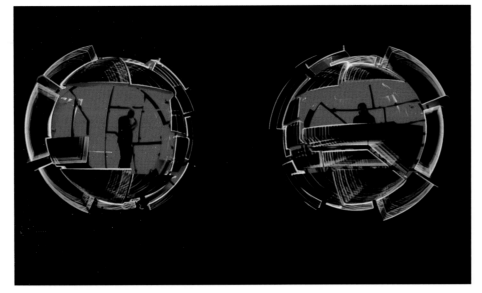

Creative Director: Heather Shaw

Production Company: Vita Motus Design Studio

Client: Infected Mushroom

Vita Motus Design Studio designed and produced the 2012 Touring Stage Experience for Infected Mushroom. The architectural intent of the design was a futuristic sculpture that visually reflects the forward thinking and innovative essences of the band. The exploded pieces making up the sphere appeared to be floating and weightless, which in essence, did succeed in conveying psychedelic and wild-style of the band. These sculptures function as individual performance pods in a variation of shapes and sizes to accommodate the artists and their activities, with the amazingly designed projection mapping to boast the 3D effect. The set rendered a mind-blowing audience experience, immersing them in a music world of color and energy. Meanwhile, animations filled the architecture in a constant state of motion that would follow the rhythm of the music.

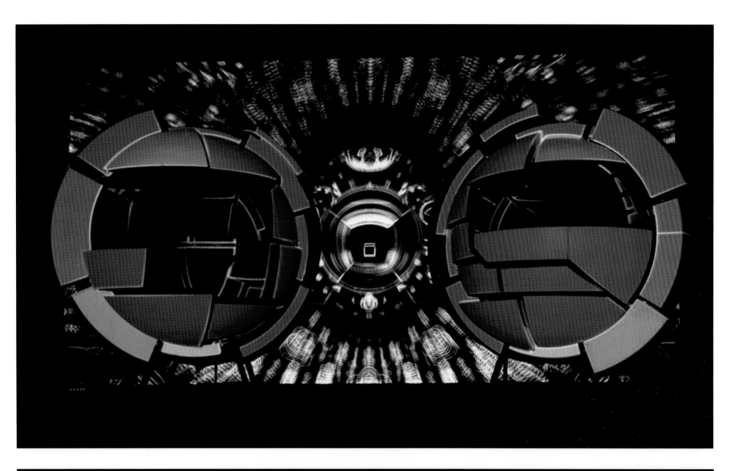

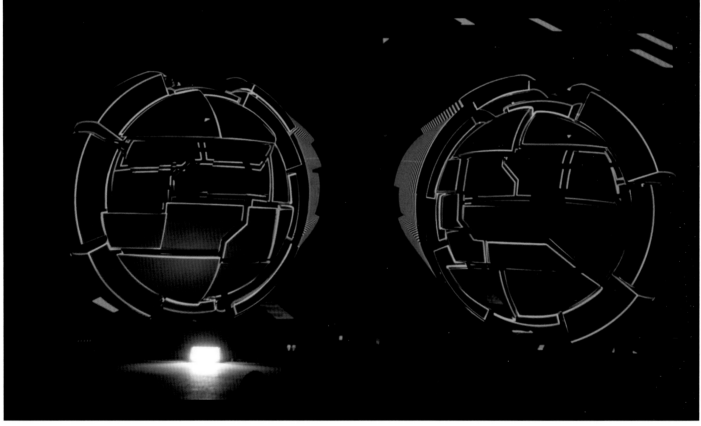

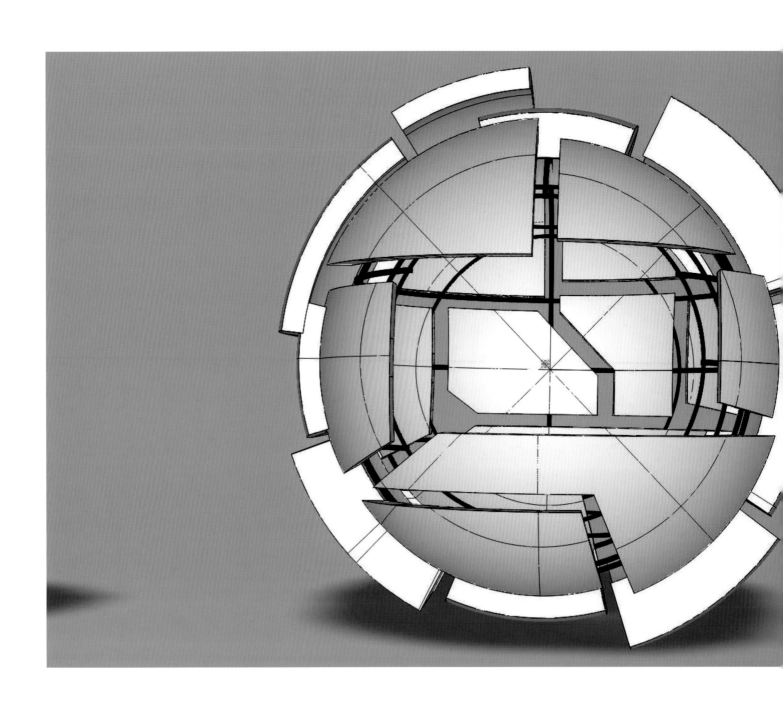

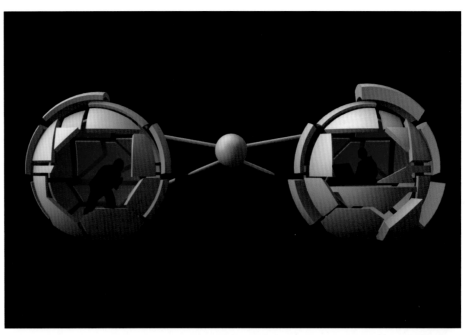

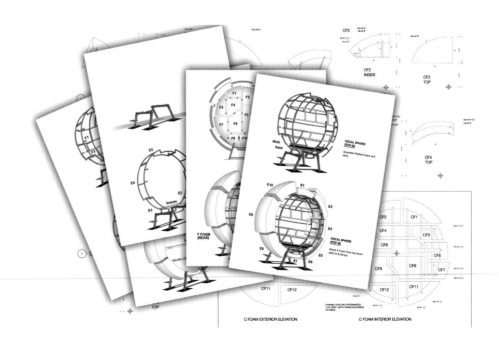

Legends of The Summer Tour

• Projection Mapping

Legends of The Summer Tour is a co-headlining concert by singers Jay-Z and Justin Timberlake to support their new studio albums. It traveled from USA to Canada and United Kingdom.

Creative Director: Willo Perron

Production Designer: Willo Perron

Assistant Creative Director: Jesse Lee Stout

Lighting Designer: Nick Whitehouse

Video Content Designer: Moment Factory

Photo Credit: Moment Factory, Anil Sharma

Content Designer: Jesse Lee Stout

After working on Jay Z's Carnegie Hall concerts in 2012, Moment Factory was mandated by Roc Nation and Willo Perron to create original video content for Jay-Z and Justin Timberlake's Legends of the Summer, one of 2013's biggest stadium tours. More than twenty different visual concepts were developed, designed to take full advantage of the massive scale of the stage. Video screens on concentric arches were set deep upstage, creating strong depth and perspective effects. Hyper-real writhing snakes, hellfire leaping skyward, and manipulated images of the artists combined to create an otherworldly atmosphere. With the creative director Willo Perron, who was responsible for the overall vision of the show, the production process was the result of a close collaboration between all members of the design team.

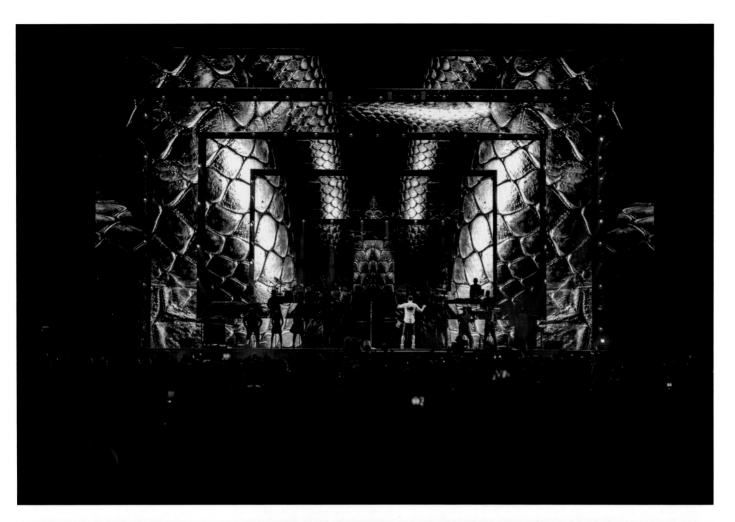

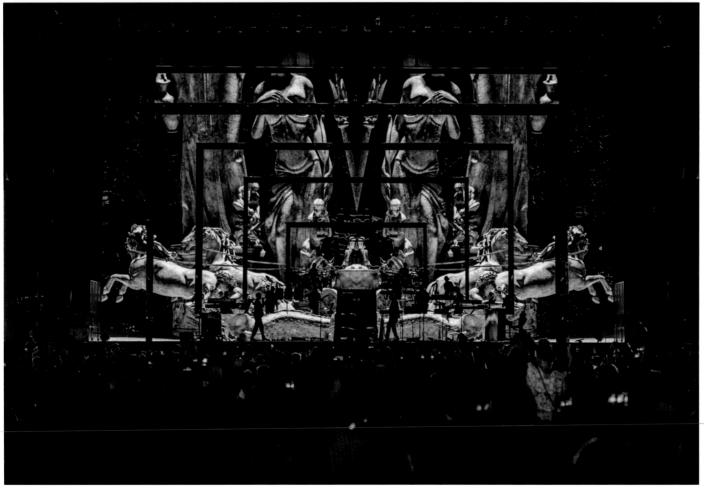

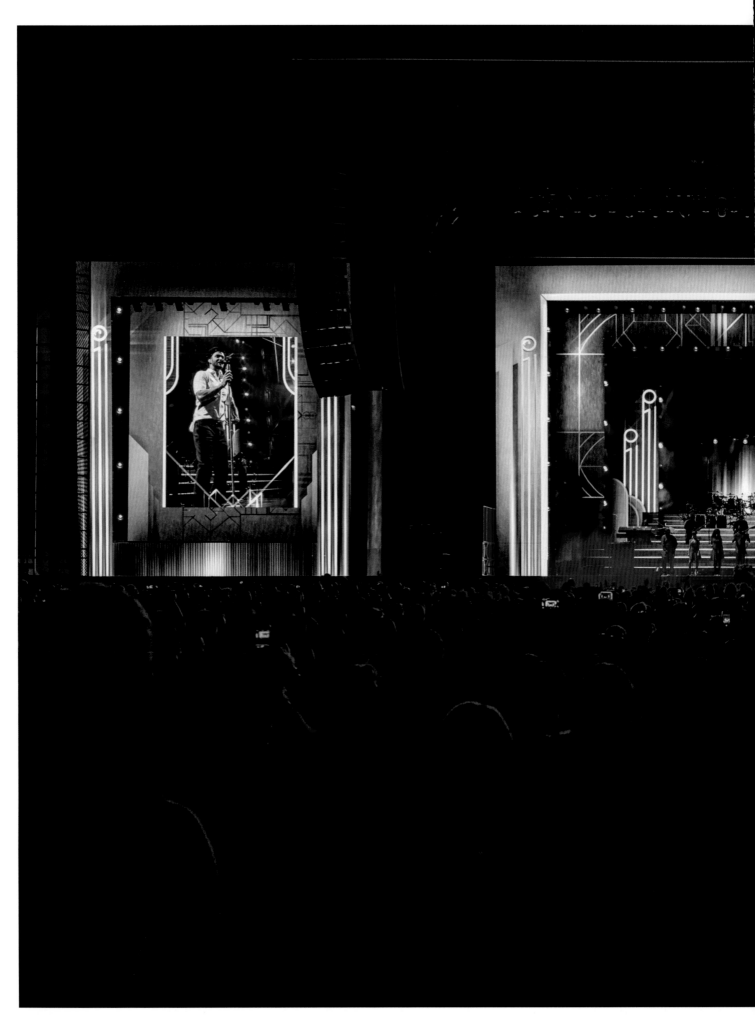

Monster Ball US Theatre Tour

• *Projection Mapping*

The Monster Ball Tour was the second global concert tour by American artist Lady Gaga which is in support of her album The Fame (2008), visiting arenas and stadiums from 2009 to 2011 all around the world. US Theatre Tour was an essential part of this tour project.

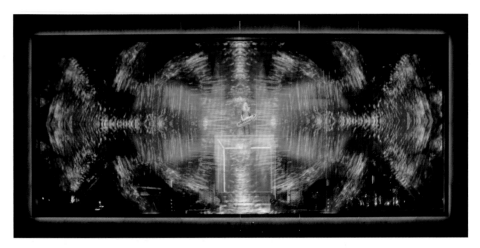

Creative Director: Haus of Gaga, Matt Williams and Willo Perron

Production Designer: Es Devlin

Choreographer: Laurie Ann Gibson

Lighting Designer: Willie Williams

Video Director: Nick Knight and Ruth Hogben

This project was originally conceived as a joint tour of Lady Gaga and Kanye West. But later, it became a solo Lady Gaga show. The design team had only 3 weeks to design the set. Under the direction of Willo Perron and the Haus, Es created an LED box with perspectives which specially showed the exquisite commissioned films by celebrated fashion photographer Nick Knight. The idea was to provide a simple yet ever-changing frame for constantly evolving work of art. That was Gaga.

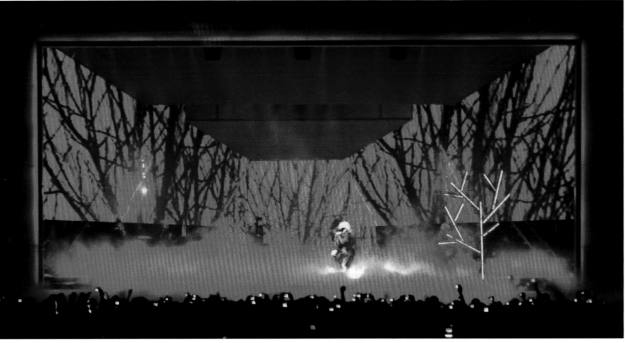

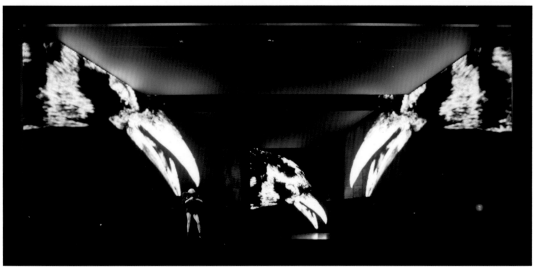

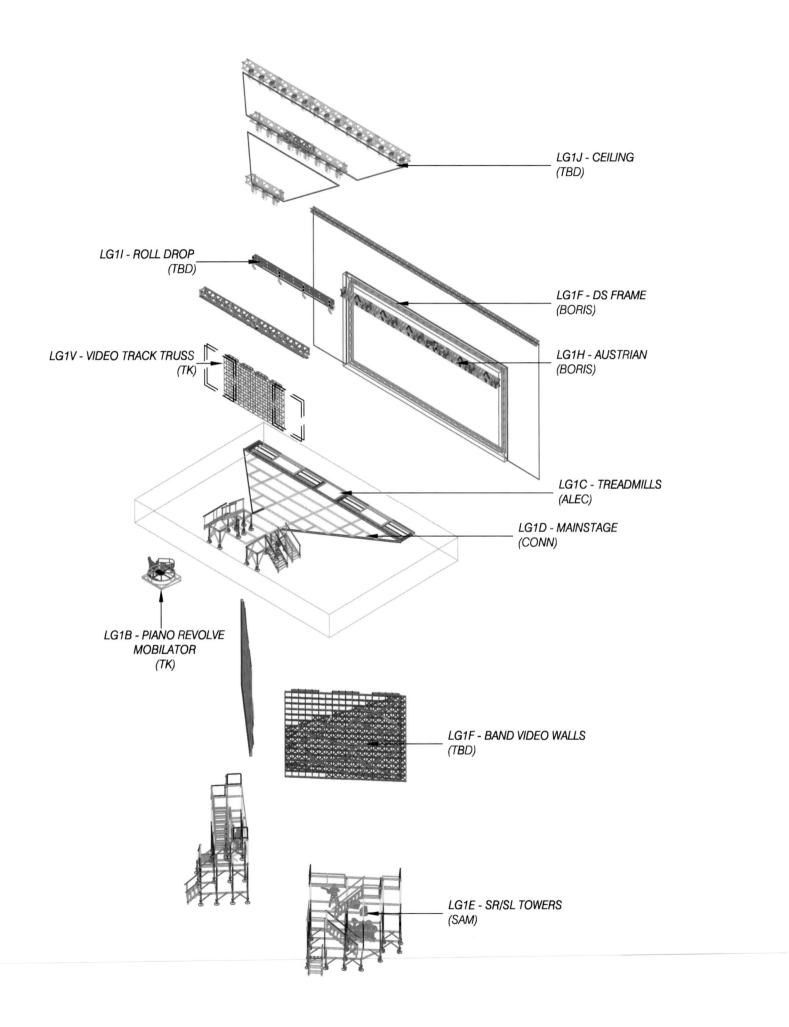

LG1J - CEILING
(TBD)

LG1I - ROLL DROP
(TBD)

LG1F - DS FRAME
(BORIS)

LG1V - VIDEO TRACK TRUSS
(TK)

LG1H - AUSTRIAN
(BORIS)

LG1C - TREADMILLS
(ALEC)

LG1D - MAINSTAGE
(CONN)

LG1B - PIANO REVOLVE
MOBILATOR
(TK)

LG1F - BAND VIDEO WALLS
(TBD)

LG1E - SR/SL TOWERS
(SAM)

Madonna's MDNA Tour

• *Multiple Video Surfaces*

In support of her twelfth studio album, Madonna's 2013 MDNA tour stopped in cities across the Americas, Europe and the Middle East.

Creative Producer: Jamie King

Show Director: Michel Laprise, Cirque du Soleil

Production Manager: Jake Berry

Show Architect: Mark Fisher

Main Video Content: Moment Factory

Other Video Content: Veneno Inc., Tom Munro,

Jonas Åkerlund, Nathan Rissman,

Johan Söderberg, Danny Tull

Video Technical Director: Stefaan Desmedt

Set Engineering and Production: Tait Towers

Choreographer: Rich Tone.

Lighting Designer: Al Gurdon

Photo Credit: Moment Factory

In collaboration with show director Michel Laprise from Cirque du Soleil, artists at Moment Factory developed a rich visual vocabulary for unique video surfaces designed by Mark Fisher, crafting a visual universe to accompany twelve different choreographies. The process required several complex animation techniques as well as the coordination of multiple video shoots in India, New York and Montreal. The dynamic stage environment took spectators on a journey deep into Madonna's artistic world. The results were richly varied: "Girl Gone Wild" was set in a photorealistic 3D cathedral; "I'm a Sinner" took the audience on a kaleidoscopic train trip through India; and the grand finale, "Celebration" was a full-throttle blast of color and movement brought to life with moving LED cubes. Every step in the rigorous production process was carried out in close collaboration with Madonna and her team.

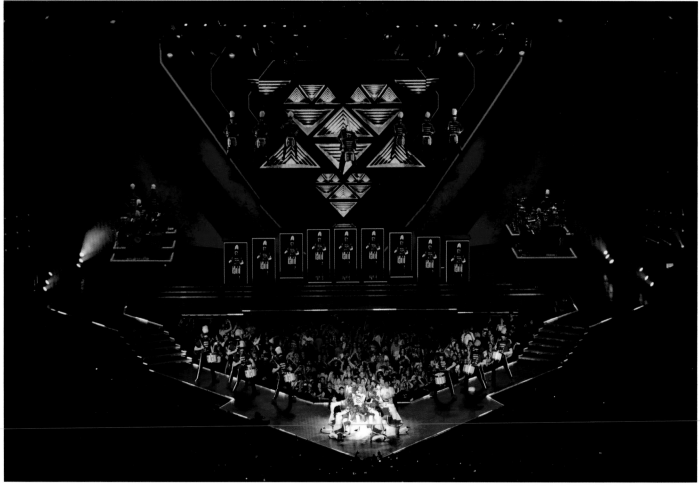

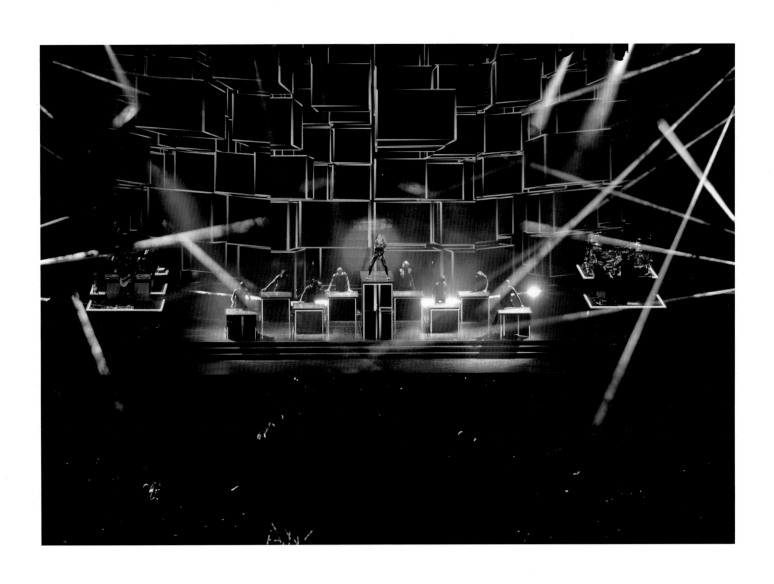

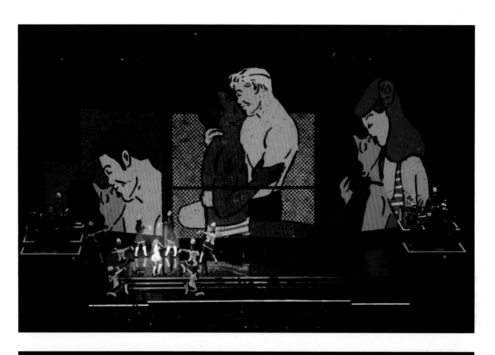

The Concert of Raptor

• Polygonal Steel Structure

The Thailand duo Raptor, Joni Anwar and Louis Scott is a well-received rap combination which has greatly shaped youthful culture in the country since the 1990s. In 1988, the duo announced "tomorrow there will be no more Raptor" in its Bangkok concert. However, thirteen years later, Joni & Louis Raptor performed Raptor 2011 at the Royal Paragon Hall in Bangkok, Thailand.

Design Company: Apostrophy's The Synthesis Server Co., Ltd.

Lighting Designer: Apostrophy's, PM Center Co.,Ltd.

Visual & Lighting Equipment: PM Center Co.,Ltd.

Art Director: Apostrophy's The Synthesis Server Co., Ltd.

Client & Organizer & Project Director: SKY-HIGH NETWORK Co.,Ltd/Cool 93 Fahrenheit

The stage started with a huge polygonal steel structure that hangs over the audience's head, generating from 3D model program in a radiant form to intimate that Raptor was back to entertain their fans again. It shaded a performance space below and spread out to the audience seating area. All of 10 steel structures were suspended in a proper position which was nine meters away to the ceiling and the floor, with each structure well studied and positioned by physical modeling. This structure was flexible to perform the variety of scenes: the exterior of the 6 wings were fabricated with white fabric, which could be used as the screen for mapping projection. Its image reflections were constantly changeable according to the mood of the music, from structure revealing to the optical art pattern, and text.

Meanwhile, the octagonal truss at the center was surrounded with LED screens, for visually ambient shows of song titles and part of lyrics, connected with the LED screen on the backdrop of the stage. To add up to the effort, the designers had used a lively color palette and light beams to boost the live stage effect such as very narrow spot, Iris scene, etc.

Finally, to focus on the stage a lifestyle of 90's teenage fashion was introduced: a huge stair case acted as the meeting point of various technologies, hydraulic platform, rotating stage and swift jumping platform, all fused into one event.

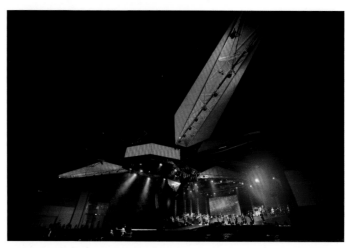

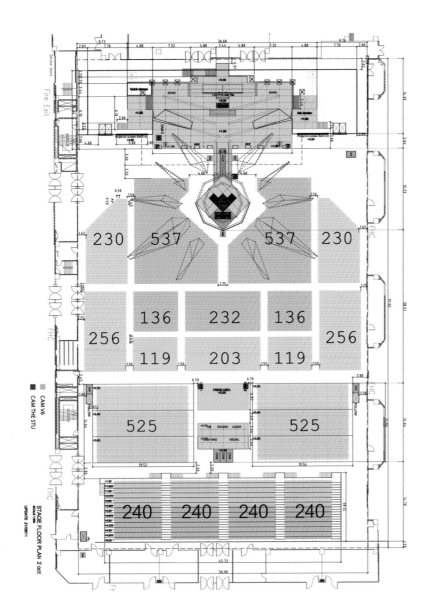

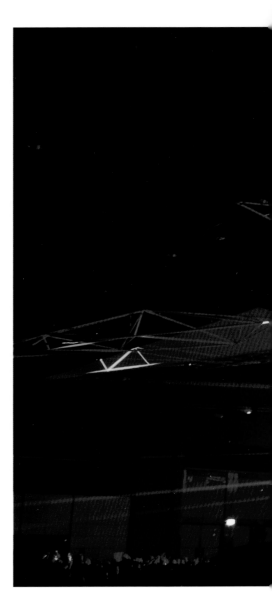

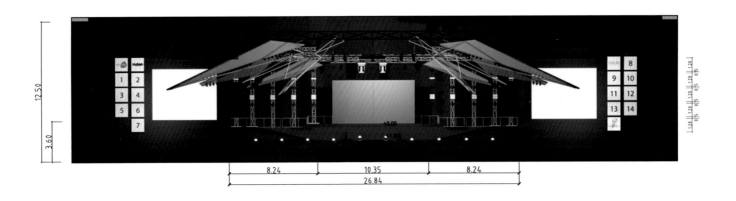

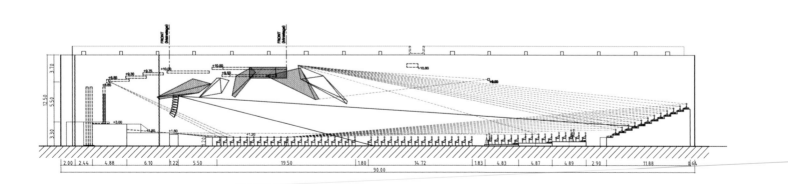

PD Radio Concert

• *Truss & Wire*

The dreamlike creation on stage integrates strength with beauty while making good use of motion graphic design.

Design Company: Apostrophy's the Synthesis server Co.,Ltd.

Client: PD Creation Co.,Ltd.

Location: Bangkok, Thailand

Apostrophy was responsible for the design and construction of the PD Radio Concert.

In construction part, this was an event, big event. With few challengeable briefs with little production lead time, Apostrophy brainstormed and decided to applied "Fast Architecture" in this project. They used Truss & Wire, combining with design and gimmick-added style. Finally, the stage became an "Installation Art". In the lighting part, addictional gimmicks always made surprises by blending with the construction part. It turned white wire into multi-colour wire, and made the atmosphere and installation extremely zestful. In the motion graphic part, each motion was specially created for each scene. Each artist, each song, and each show had their own fascinating uniqueness of motion graphic contents.

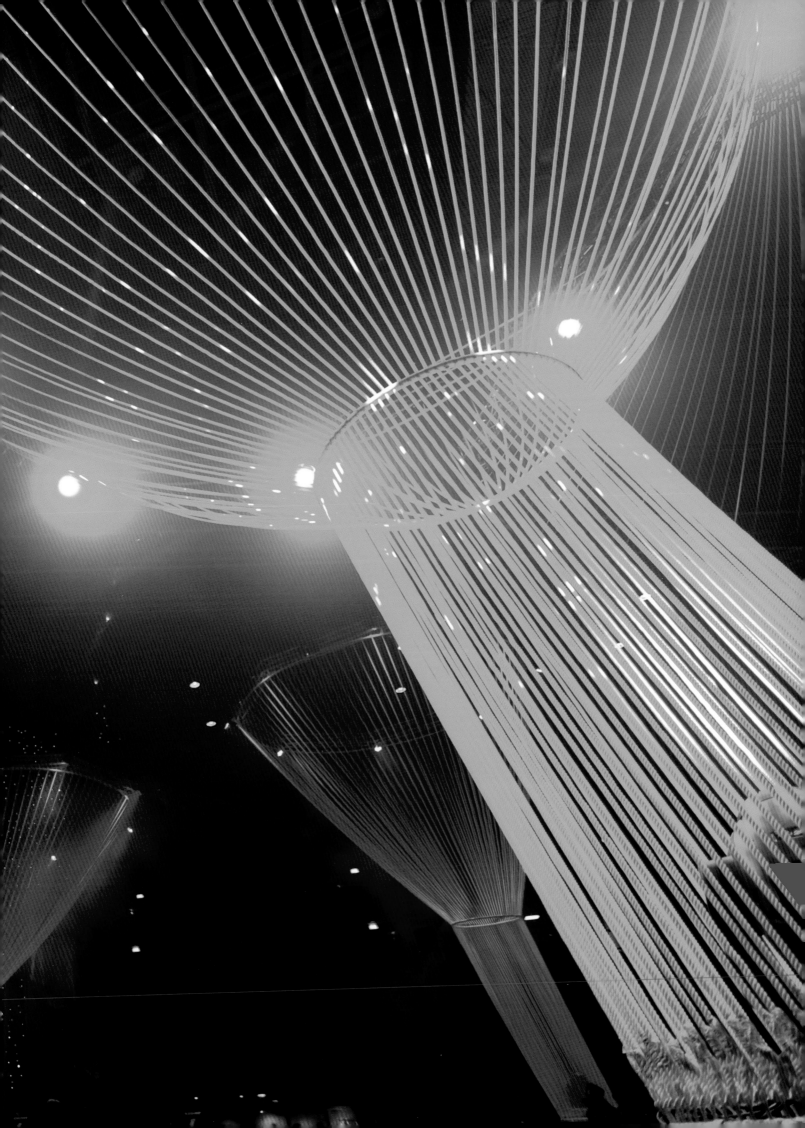

EVENTS & CEREMONIES

The key of the stage design for events and ceremonies is the creation of mental aura. In general, "mental aura" is an integration of the theme and idea of the stage, stage art performance, and the audience's aesthetic feelings etc, which is the soul of the whole event or ceremony.

Mental aura cannot be done without installations and digital technologies. In the past few decades, installation art and digital technologies have experienced their development with historic significance. They are used in almost every part of the design process for the events and ceremonies by stage designers, including audio design, lighting design, scenery and visual effects. With the help of flexible applications of various technologies and the aura, the stage will present a delightful performance for the audiences, as well as the theme and artistic style.

Beijing Olympic Games Opening Ceremony

• Movable Type Press

The 2008 Olympic Games opening ceremony was held in the Beijing National Stadium, also known as the Bird's Nest. The artistic part of the ceremony consisted of two parts titled "Brilliant Civilization" and "Glorious Era" respectively. This project, involved in the first part, highlighted the Chinese civilization and extended to modern China with dream of harmony for the world.

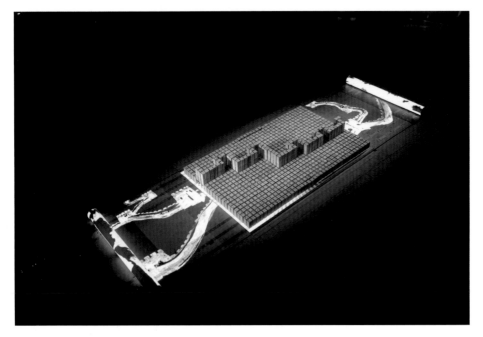

Designer: Lixun Han

Design Company: Han's Studio

Client: Beijing Organizing Committee for the Olympic Games

During the procedure, a giant scroll was moved aside to show a fluid array of 897 movable type-blocks which formed three variations of the Chinese character ' 和 ', meaning harmony, in Bronze Inscription, Seal script and Kai Script (Modern Chinese Script). It is one of the greatest Chinese ancient inventions–the movable type press. Performers in Zhou-era style mimicked the "3,000 Disciples of Confucius" and held bamboo slips. They recited some excerpts from The Analects, "All the people of the world are brothers". Soon, the blocks transformed into a miniature Great Wall, then into plum blossoms, a Chinese symbol of openness. At the end of the sequence, all tops of the movable type blocks came off, while 897 performers revealed and waved vigorously to the crowds, to surprise them that such changeable performance had been realized by no computer monitoring and synchronizing but a result of the co-effort of real human performers.

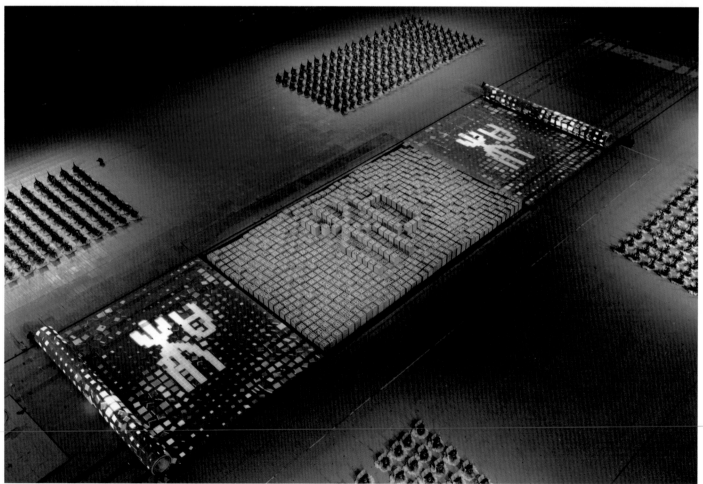

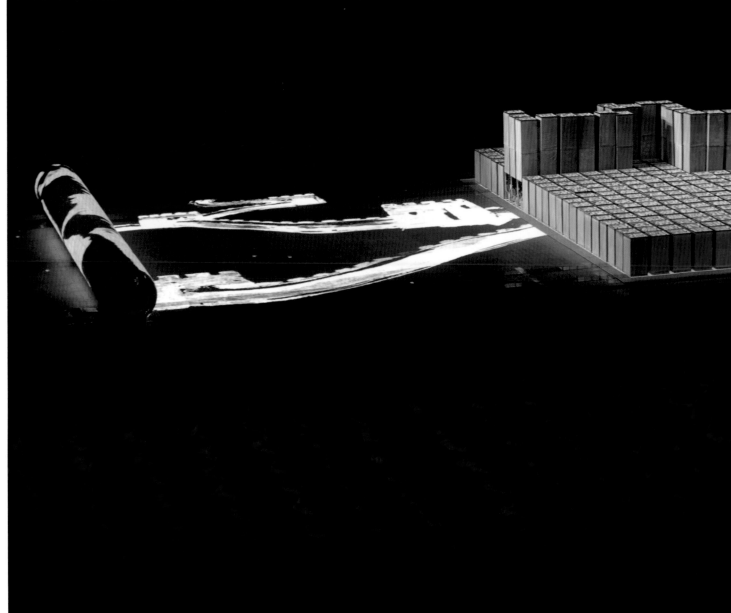

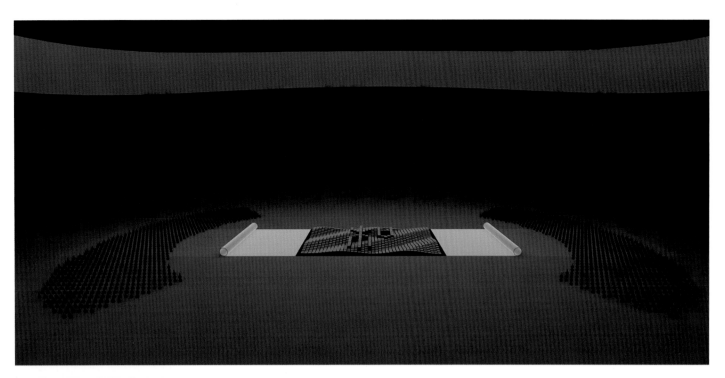

字模—画—四边处理制作参考

红色范围以外向下包住字模侧面
技术上要求：展开时要平整，
要能够快速收回

放大

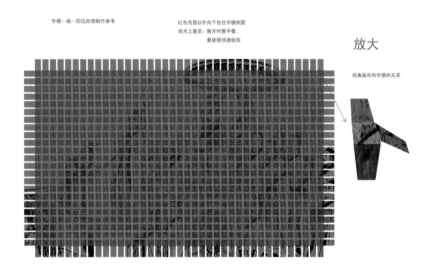

四角画布和字模的关系

字——制作图

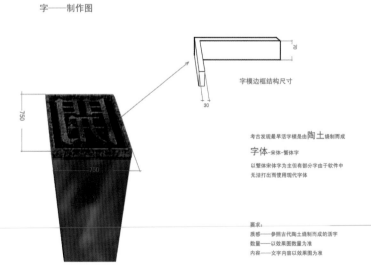

字模边框结构尺寸

考古发现最早活字模是由 陶土 烧制而成

字体-宋体-繁体字

以繁体宋体字为主但有部分字由于软件中
无法打出而使用现代字体

要求：
质感——参照古代陶土烧制而成的活字
数量——以效果图数量为准
内容——文字内容以效果图为准

The Coachella Valley
Music & Arts Festival

• *The Immersive Installation*

The Coachella Valley Music and Arts Festival is an annual three-day music and arts festival, founded by Paul Tollett, and held at the Empire Polo Club in Indio, California in the Inland Empire's Coachella Valley. It covers a wide range of music genres and live music on several stages — Coachella Stage, Outdoor Theatre, Gobi Tent, Mojave Tent, and the Sahara Tent.

Creative Director: Josh Flemming

Art Director: Heather Shaw

Design Companies: The Do LaB, Vita Motus Design Studio

Client: Coachella Valley Music and Arts Festival

Designers Josh Flemming from The Do LaB and Heather Shaw from Vita Motus Design Studio teamed up for the ninth year to design a 360 degree immersive environment for the festival, including shade structures, DJ stage and a video and water performance installation. The goal of this acre-wide installation was to create a massive whimsical environment that served many functional needs as well as to lure in audience from local and remote places. The periphery was lined with six colorful tents that were catching and efficient in providing maximum shade in the desert sun. A center cloud sculpture was mounted as a misting video installation and a 360-degree dance performance stage. By day the cloud misted and cooled down the overheated participants of the festival and at night the ever-changing video and light effect transported the audience into another dimension.

EVENTS & CEREMONIES

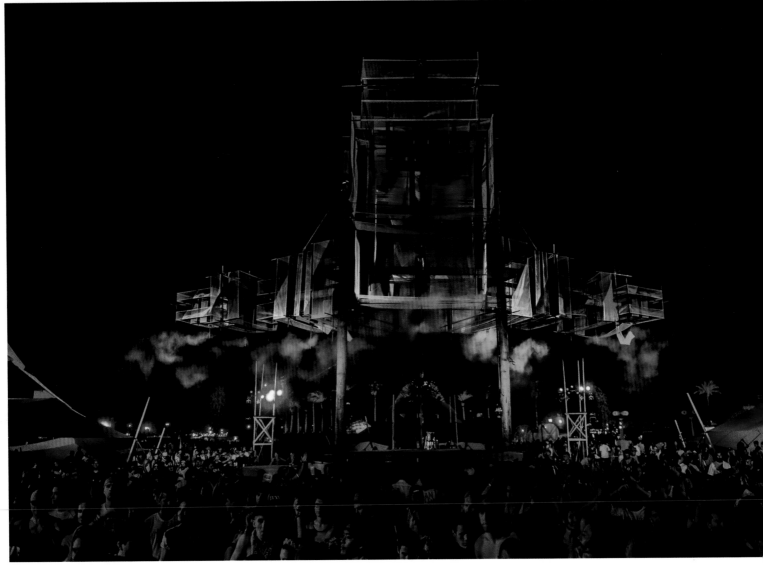

· The Impressive Concepts of Coachella 2013 ·

— The Do Lab and Coachella

As an annual two-weekend, and three-day music and art festival, the Coachella Valley Music and Arts Festival had been projecting visual arts since the first year it had been established. The festival featured installation art and sculptures in addition to pop music every year. The Do Lab has gained a reputation by its development and creation of art installations and stages in large scale. Numerous outstanding artists, including The Glitch Mob and Bassnecter, had subsequently highlighted Coachella's dance music focused Sahara tent, making the Do Lab stage a place to watch for new musical talents.

— The immersive installation

In the ninth successive year, the soul and heart of the Coachella Valley Music and

Arts Festival had been shaped and decorated by both The Do LaB and Lucent Dossier Experience in 2013. The crafted immersive installation designed and made by The Do LaB was a florid masterpiece. The landscape of The Empire Polo Fields is a flat acre with unobstructed grass. By disrupting this ground plane, the installation created conditions with high and low, above and below, near and far, flat and sloped elements, all of which were the places that could not be experienced in other events but here.

The installation immersed Coachella attendees in revitalizing water and movement which was inspired electronic music. The Do Lab's vision for their Coachella stage was perfectly suited for the site and theme of the festival. The 100-feet long, 80 foot wide art "Mirage" was erected on the place behind the main stage which was envisioned by the art designer Paul Clemente. Taking the inspiration from the architecture of a mid-century, he designed the installation. With 21 projectors, images were displayed on the white wall and floors, which were changing throughout the night. In the middle, there was a projected pool in high-definition clarity with such details that made you almost forget it was a projection and want to jump in after a long day sweating in the desert.

Most pieces of the installations were interactive, providing a visual treat for the attendees walking throughout the site. Some of the works have also been featured at Burning Man and Art Basel, involved participants from the local architecture local and international schools.

Above all are the essence of designs and installation of the Coachella, which gave texture and unique characteristics to the overall Coachella 2013.

The 50th Anniversary of Allianz Global Investors

• Media Ribbon Sculpture

Allianz is a German multinational financial services company headquartered in Munich, with insurance as its core business. The 50th anniversary of Allianz Global Investors was held a major concert hall in the Alte Oper, a original opera house in Frankfurt, to acquire a futurist-oriented environment for the event, as well as to honor the company's tradition.

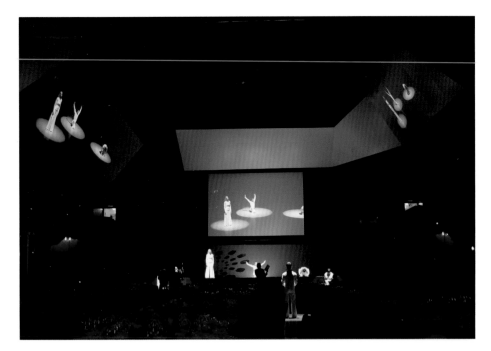

Stage Designer: Boris Banozic

Production Company: Quasar Communications

Client: dit—Allianz Global Investors

Photo Credit: Jürgen Zeller

The large media-played ribbons starting from the stage created a three-dimensional sculpture that stretched to the back of the hall, wrapping the audience in the center. This eliminated the distance between the audience and the stage. It converted them into actors and fully emerged them in the situation. Theses unfolding ribbons, with their smooth transitions and rising format associated with the curve of rising share prices, deliberately played with the optical perception and recipient visual patterns. During the artistic and cinematic interpretations of dit history and themes, a great variety of sequences had been developed through the dynamic geometry of the projection screens, inviting the guests onto a holistic journey.

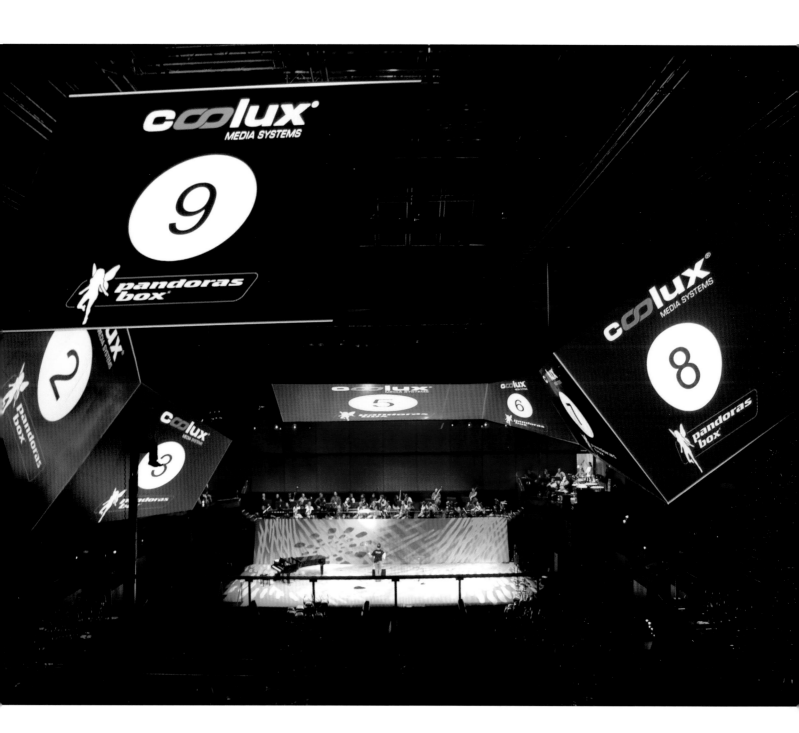

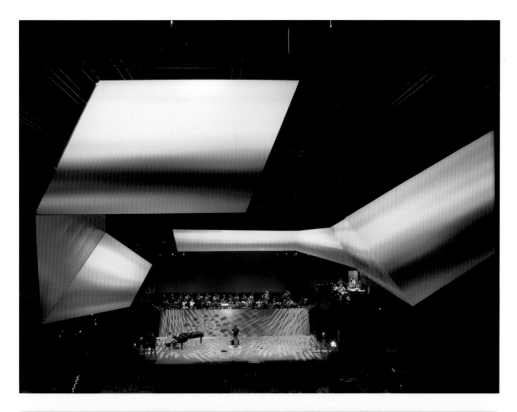

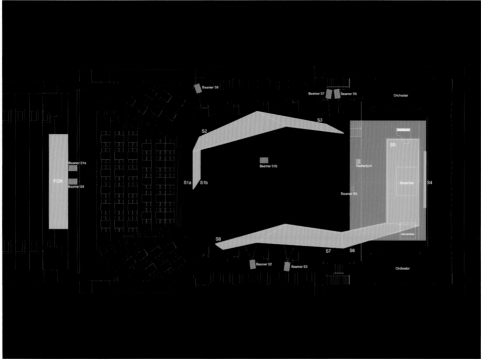

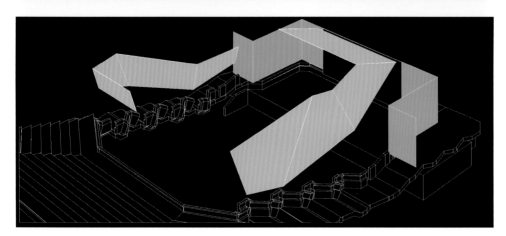

Make It Right

• Angular Lines + Projection Mapping

Founded by celebrity Brad Pitt and designer William McDonough in 2007, Make It Right builds healthy homes and buildings for American communities in need. The organization started with rebuilding homes in New Orleans after Hurricane Katrina and is currently working in New Orleans, LA, Newark, NJ and Kansas City, MO. They also create Library and Laboratory for knowledge sharing.

Design

Production Designer: Stefan Beese, RE:BE Design

Production Company: Rehage Entertainment

Stage Designer: Stefun Beese

Client: Make It Right Foundation (MIR)

Gala

Audio Gala: Swank Audio

Video Gala: The Solomon Group

Video Engineer: Jonathan Foucheaux & Scott Bufford

LED Technician: Jay Taylor

Imag Screens: Swank Audio

Lighting Gala: The Soloman Group

Lighting Director: Jonathan Foucheaux

Set Builder: John Himmaugh and Co

After Party

Lighting Arrival & Performance: See Hear Productions

Lighting Director: Patrick Theriot

Audio: VER Audio

Cameras: YES productions

Rigging: Corporate Lighting and Audio

To achieve a unique stage for this charity gala, Production Designer, Stefan Beese, utilized both angular and overlapping lines from the Make It Right houses which were recently built, along with the "Front Porch" which is with cultural significance of NOLA. Both of them needed to be tied together with the three major staging areas as required: a performance area for Sheryl Crow and Rihanna, a location for Ellen DeGeneres' interviews with Brad Pitt and MIR family members, as well as a stage location where the gala would be hosted. Thus, it was important to create a set which would fuse the functionality of a TV set, an award show and a performance stage all into one. The final solution would use a 15mm video wall as the farthest upstage layer, masked by physical set pieces that framed the LED wall. This physical set formed the walls to compensate the first upstage layers and the second layer. It served as the projection surfaces for video mapping content—the primary design element for the gala stage.

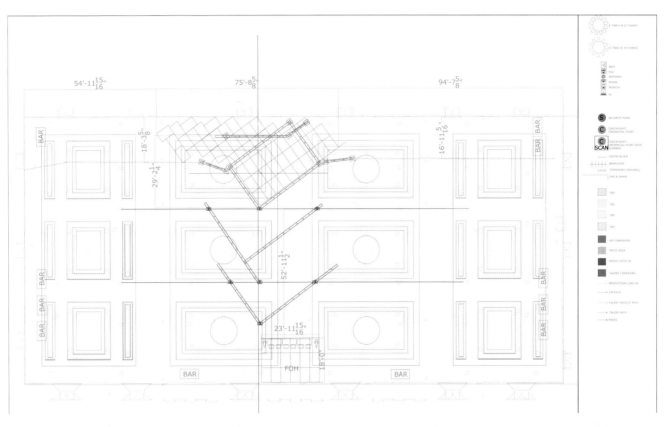

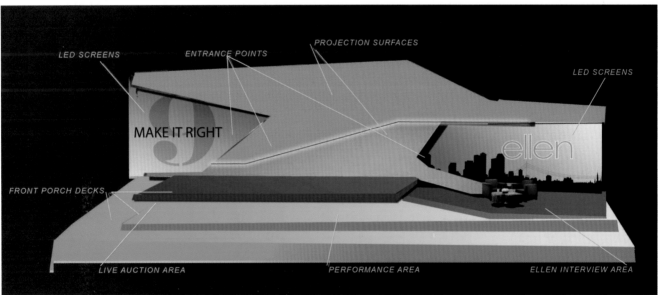

LED SCREENS   ENTRANCE POINTS   PROJECTION SURFACES

LED SCREENS

MAKE IT RIGHT

ellen

FRONT PORCH DECKS

LIVE AUCTION AREA   PERFORMANCE AREA   ELLEN INTERVIEW AREA

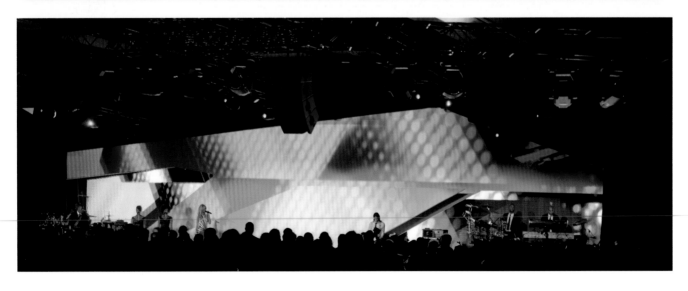

American Idol Season 11 & 12

• Ribbon Panels

American Idol is an American reality singing competition program. It is one of the most successful shows in the history of American television. For eight consecutive unprecedented years from the 4th season in 2003 to the 11th season in 2010, both its performance and resulting show had been ranked as number one in U.S. television ratings.

Creative Director: Heather Shaw

Art Director: David Edwards

Design Company: Vita Motus Design Studio, Heather Shaw Production Design

Client: American Idol

This set design breathed new life into this 11-year old show, adding sweeping lines, a clean and sophisticated environment and exciting new technologies to the stage where 24 contestants battled for America's vote for the 13 weeks of airing. The design featured an oval LED wall which was splited into six separate panels behind the contestants, each of which opened and rotated in either direction. Most impressive thing was the clean design style, which themed with the movement to allow for three-dimensional media mapping, from the ceiling to the floor. At any moment, the entire set can be fully and visually transformed to meet the ever-changing moods and emotions of the musical performance and live television.

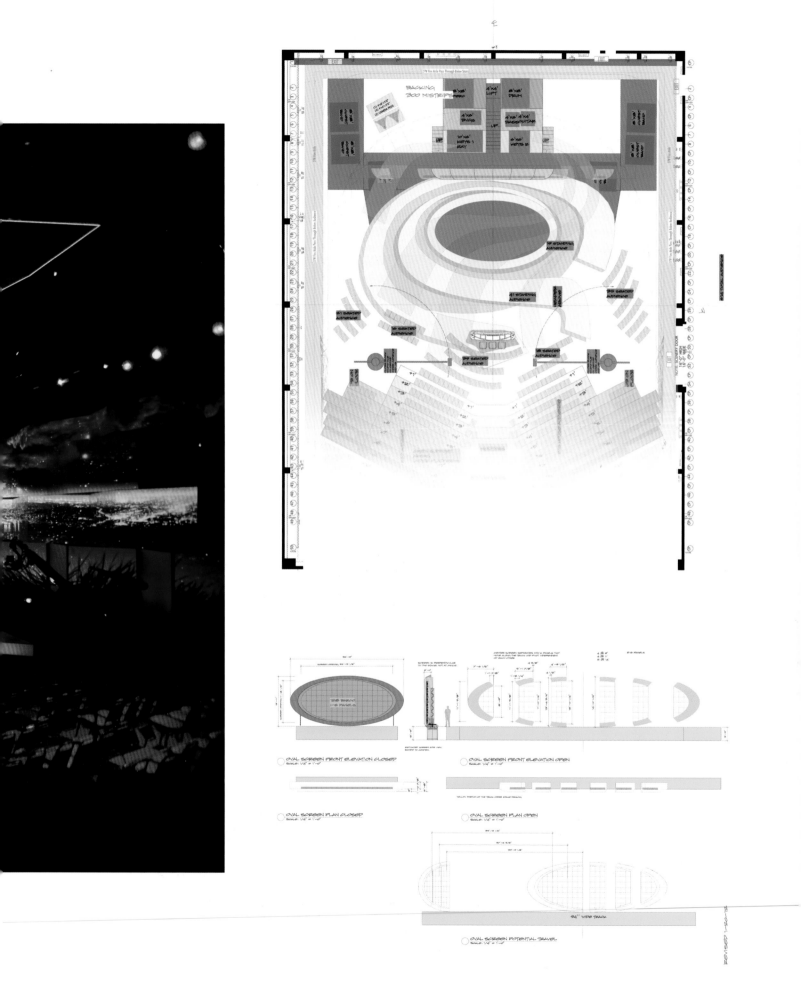

The 10th Anniversary Celebration of Berlin Jewish Museum

• Sculpture Stage

The Jewish Museum Berlin is one of the largest Jewish and the most frequented Museums in Europe. In its two buildings, German-Jewish history is documented in the collections, library and archive in the computer terminals at the museum's Rafael Roth Learning Center reflected in the museum's program of events.

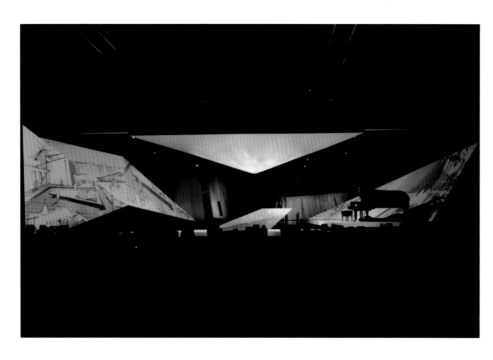

Creative Director: Boris Banozic, Jan Hennings (VOK DAMS)

Art Director: Daniel Bandke

Stage Designer: Boris Banozic

Client: Jewish Museum Berlin, VOK DAMS

The former Flower Market Hall opposite to the museum accommodating the new Academy of the museum, was chosen for the venue. The stage was like a window that opened the view to the construction site of the future Academy. The composition of triangular shapes is arranged to form the Roman numeral of 10, marking the museum's history. The projection screens glued the audience's views to the background by recapping photographs from the past ten years of exhibitions and events. The staging evolved a media-architectonic time line from the past to the future.

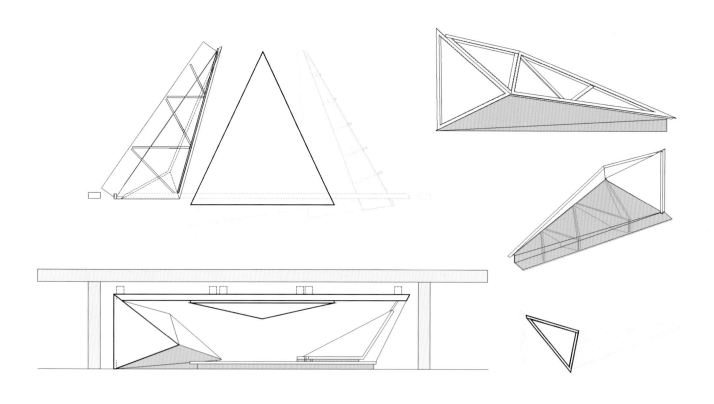

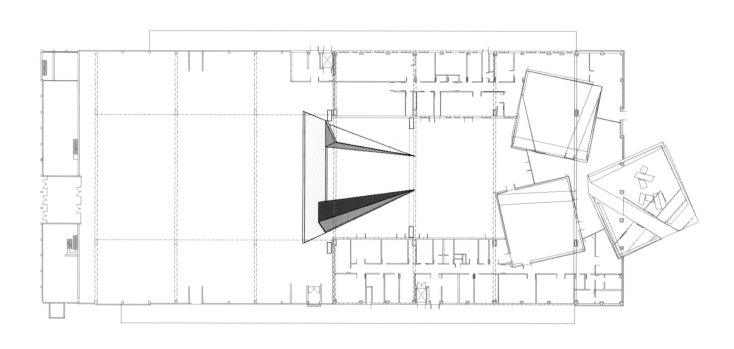

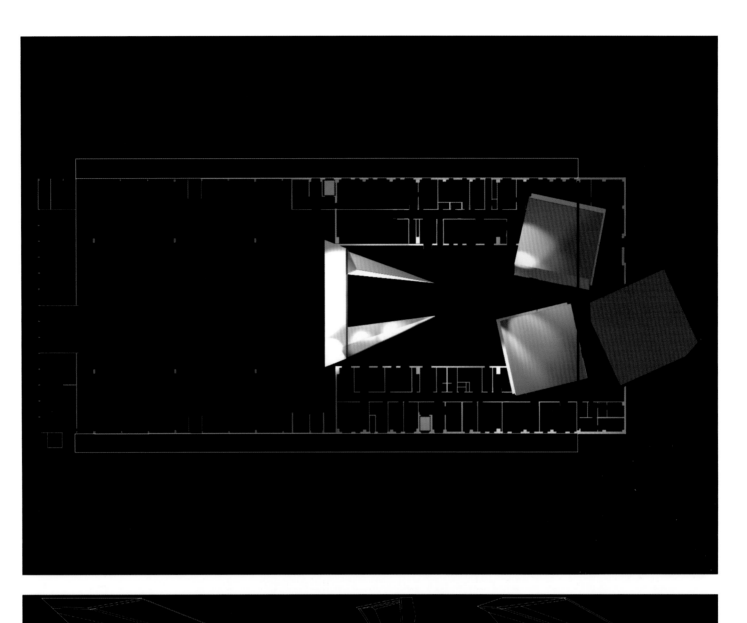

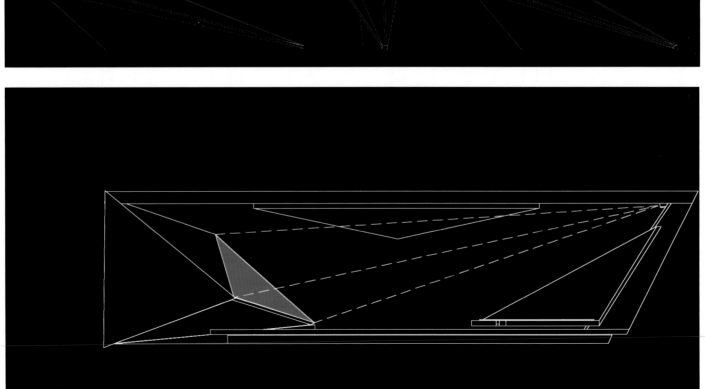

Bethlehem Christmas

• Landscaped Stage

Bethlehem is a Palestinian city neighbouring Jerusalem, which is recognized by the New Testament as the birthplace of Jesus and home to one of the largest Palestinian Christian communities. It has been a Christmas preference for Christians all around the world, providing various religious activities in the holiday season, like processions, special church services etc.

Creative Director/Stage Designer: Chad Ellenburg

Art Director: Joe Welch

Creative Team: Chad Ellenburg, Joe Welch, Kara Welch, Greg Lossen

Client: Pleasant Valley Church

This Bethlehem stage design created a street scene in the first century of Bethlehem for Pleasant Valley Church. Stage Designer Chad Ellenburg wanted to landscape the stage set to be a street view for the congregation. He used a projected digital backdrop, detailing a hillside scene with a road stretching into the distance and using perspectives from the buildings on both sides of the central stage to create a sense of depth and scale.

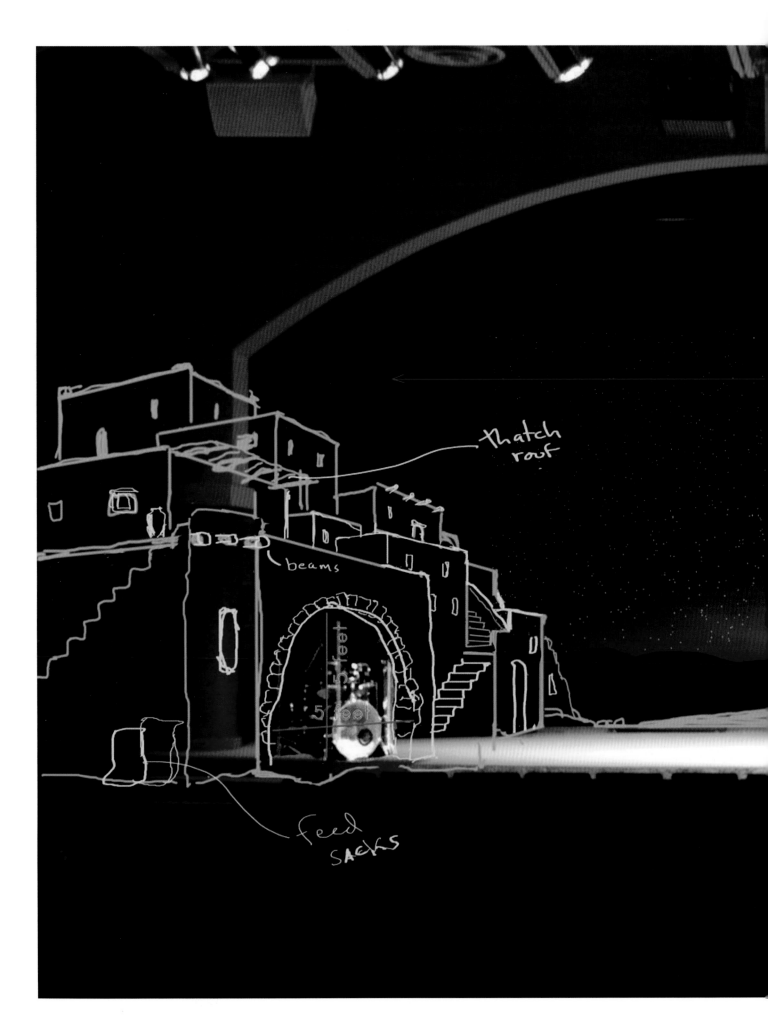

Home for Christmas

• Ribbon Background

The show was a TV Christmas special on PBS stations, which began on Nov. 30th, 2013. It featured Ireland's best female musicians, the lineup of which has changed over the years. It reached out to worldwide audience via television and international tours and won multi-platinum album sales in many countries.

Producers: Maggie Seidel, Ned O'Hanlon

Creative Director: Russell Thomas

Musical Director: David Downes

Stage Director/Choreographer: Daryn Crosbie

Set Designer: Matt Deely

Lighting Designer: Al Gurdon

Costume Designer: Synan O'Mahony

Video content Designer: Ian Reith

Photo credit: Kip Carroll

The set consists of a black, shiny dance floor, two orchestra platforms and a choir platform. Across in the back there were three ribbon-shaped scenic elements and a star cloth. There were images projected onto the scenic ribbons throughout the show, reflecting a warm Christmas atmosphere.

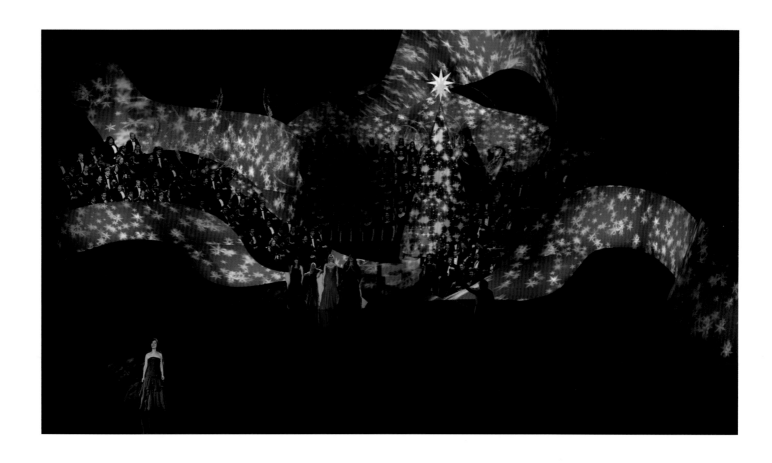

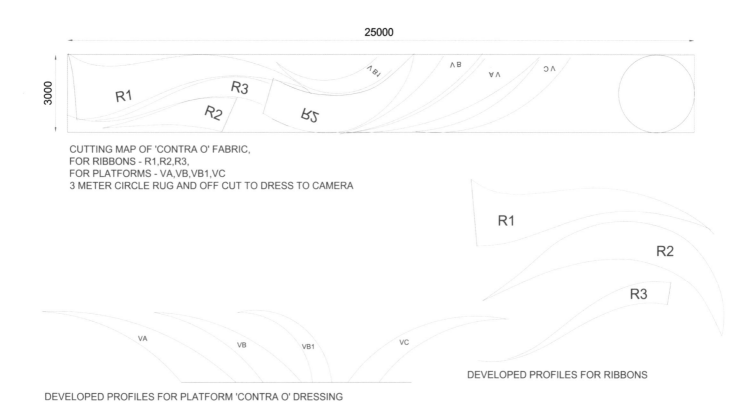

CUTTING MAP OF 'CONTRA O' FABRIC,
FOR RIBBONS - R1,R2,R3,
FOR PLATFORMS - VA,VB,VB1,VC
3 METER CIRCLE RUG AND OFF CUT TO DRESS TO CAMERA

DEVELOPED PROFILES FOR RIBBONS

DEVELOPED PROFILES FOR PLATFORM 'CONTRA O' DRESSING

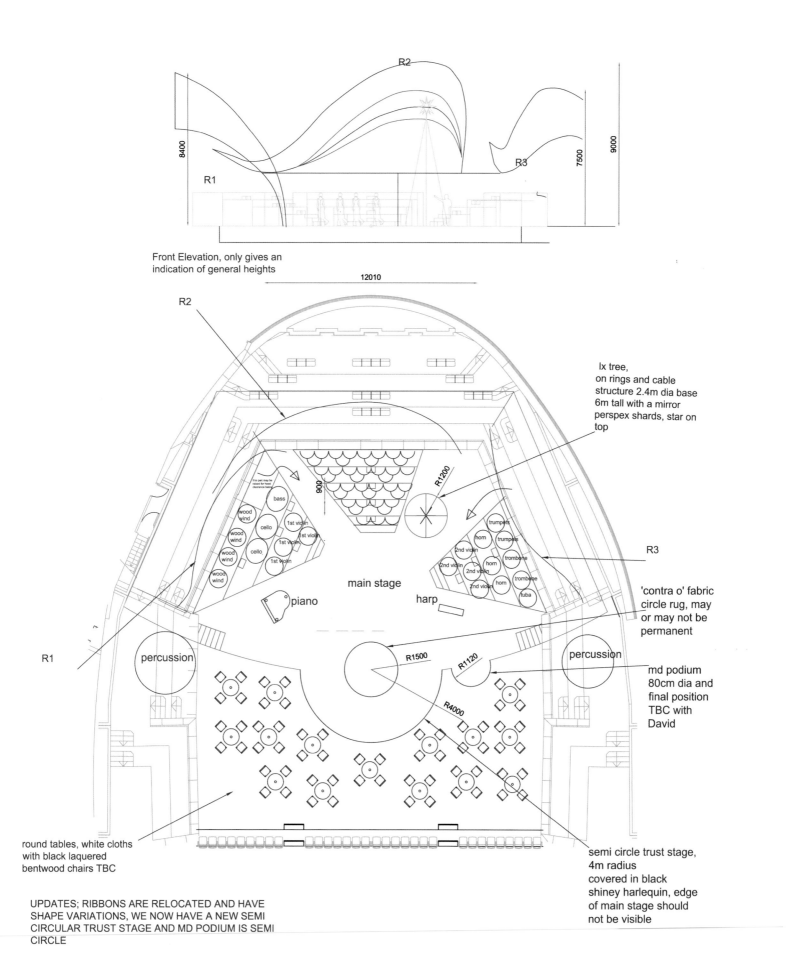

R2

8400

9000

7500

R1

R3

Front Elevation, only gives an
indication of general heights

12010

R2

lx tree,
on rings and cable
structure 2.4m dia base
6m tall with a mirror
perspex shards, star on
top

900

R1200

bass

wood
wind

cello

1st violin

wood
wind

1st violin

cello

1st violin

wood
wind

trumpets

horn

trumpets

2nd violin

trombone

2nd violin

horn

2nd violin

horn

trombone

2nd violin

tuba

R3

wood
wind

main stage

harp

'contra o' fabric
circle rug, may
or may not be
permanent

piano

percussion

R1

R1500

R1120

percussion

md podium
80cm dia and
final position
TBC with
David

R4000

round tables, white cloths
with black laquered
bentwood chairs TBC

semi circle trust stage,
4m radius
covered in black
shiney harlequin, edge
of main stage should
not be visible

UPDATES; RIBBONS ARE RELOCATED AND HAVE
SHAPE VARIATIONS, WE NOW HAVE A NEW SEMI
CIRCULAR TRUST STAGE AND MD PODIUM IS SEMI
CIRCLE

The 15th Essence Music Festival

• Curved LED Wall + Framed Screens

The Essence Music Festival is the largest event celebrating African-American culture and music in the United States. It has been held in New Orleans, Louisiana every year since 1995, except for 2006 due to Hurricane Katrina. In 2009, it celebrated its 15th anniversary with top performers including Beyonce, Lionel Richie, Anita Baker, Ne-Yo, John Legend, and Maxwell.

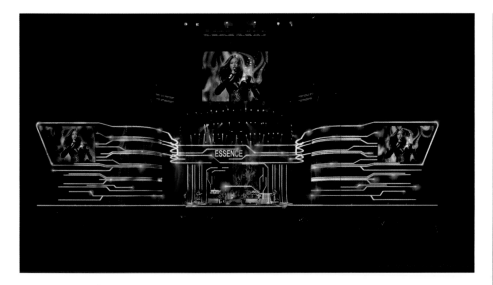

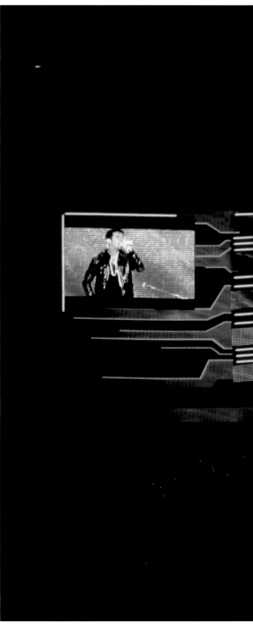

Production Designer: Stefan Beese, RE: BE Design

3D Designer: Seyavash Zohoori

Video Lighting Designer: Ray Zeigler

Set Lighting Designer: John Clarke

Client: Essence Communications Inc.

The stage design showed the significance of this recurrent festival with celebratory imagery in a digital time tracing format. Versa Tubes were chosen as the vessels for this light traveling appearance, with light strokes fading in and out, to create a circuit-board-like effect. The curved LED walls and the frames around screens would make the stage more readable as one cohesive sculpture, opposing to an arrangement of single video components, which could be comprehended smoothly, horizontally and vertically.

Production designer Stefan Beese singled out the vignette for every artist by finding a specific element to emphasize the individual style of a musician to accomplish the festival identity without taking away from the individual glamour of the artists, such as a digital rain backdrop for Ne-Yo and a candlelight atmosphere for John Legend.

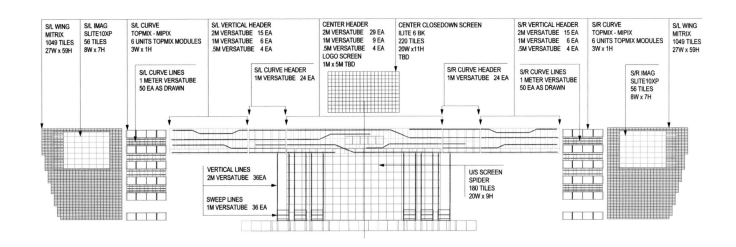

| S/L WING MITRIX 1049 TILES 27W x 59H | S/L IMAG SLITE10XP 56 TILES 8W x 7H | S/L CURVE TOPMIX - MIPIX 6 UNITS TOPMIX MODULES 3W x 1H | S/L VERTICAL HEADER 2M VERSATUBE 15 EA 1M VERSATUBE 6 EA .5M VERSATUBE 4 EA | CENTER HEADER 2M VERSATUBE 29 EA 1M VERSATUBE 9 EA .5M VERSATUBE 4 EA LOGO SCREEN 1M x 5M TBD | CENTER CLOSEDOWN SCREEN ILITE 6 BK 220 TILES 20W x11H TBD | S/R VERTICAL HEADER 2M VERSATUBE 15 EA 1M VERSATUBE 6 EA .5M VERSATUBE 4 EA | S/R CURVE TOPMIX - MIPIX 6 UNITS TOPMIX MODULES 3W x 1H | S/L WING MITRIX 1049 TILES 27W x 59H |

S/L CURVE LINES
1 METER VERSATUBE
50 EA AS DRAWN

S/L CURVE HEADER
1M VERSATUBE 24 EA

S/R CURVE HEADER
1M VERSATUBE 24 EA

S/R CURVE LINES
1 METER VERSATUBE
50 EA AS DRAWN

S/R IMAG
SLITE10XP
56 TILES
8W x 7H

VERTICAL LINES
2M VERSATUBE 36EA

SWEEP LINES
1M VERSATUBE 36 EA

U/S SCREEN
SPIDER
180 TILES
20W x 9H

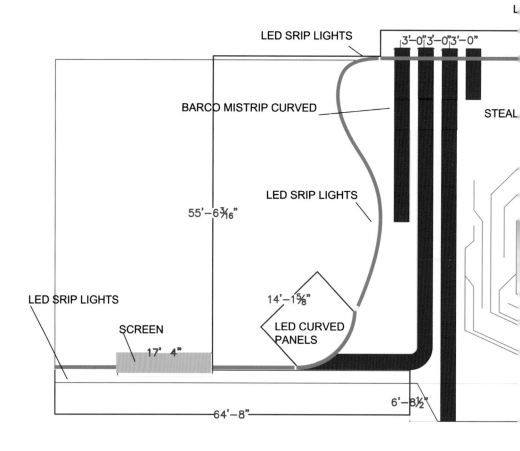

LED SRIP LIGHTS

BARCO MISTRIP CURVED

STEAL

LED SRIP LIGHTS

55'-6 3/16"

14'-1 5/8"

LED CURVED
PANELS

LED SRIP LIGHTS

SCREEN

17' 4"

64'-8"

6'-8 1/2"

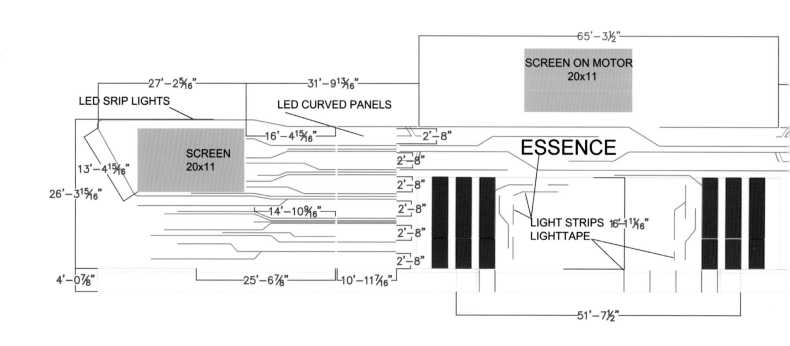

65'-3 1/2"

SCREEN ON MOTOR
20x11

27'-2 5/16"

31'-9 13/16"

LED SRIP LIGHTS

LED CURVED PANELS

16'-4 15/16"

2'-8"

ESSENCE

13'-4 15/16"

SCREEN
20x11

2'-8"

2'-8"

26'-3 15/16"

2'-8"

14'-10 9/16"

2'-8"

LIGHT STRIPS 16'-1 11/16"

LIGHTTAPE

2'-8"

4'-0 7/8"

25'-6 7/8"

10'-11 7/16"

51'-7 1/2"

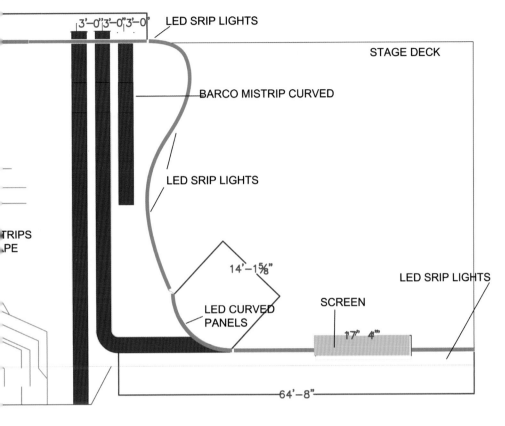

'S

LED SRIP LIGHTS

3'-0' 3'-0" 3'-0'

STAGE DECK

BARCO MISTRIP CURVED

LED SRIP LIGHTS

TRIPS
PE

14'-1⅝"

LED CURVED
PANELS

SCREEN

LED SRIP LIGHTS

17" 4"

64'-8"

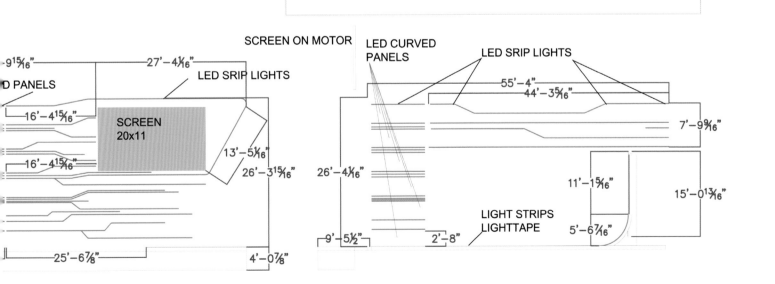

SCREEN ON MOTOR

LED CURVED
PANELS

LED SRIP LIGHTS

9¹⁵⁄₁₆"

27'-4¹⁄₁₆"

55'-4"

LED SRIP LIGHTS

44'-3⁵⁄₁₆"

D PANELS

16'-4¹⁵⁄₁₆"

SCREEN
20x11

7'-9⁹⁄₁₆"

13'-5¹⁄₁₆"

16'-4¹⁵⁄₁₆"

26'-3¹⁵⁄₁₆"

26'-4¹⁄₁₆"

11'-1⁹⁄₁₆"

15'-0¹³⁄₁₆"

LIGHT STRIPS
LIGHTTAPE

5'-6⁷⁄₁₆"

25'-6⁷⁄₈"

4'-0⁷⁄₈"

9'-5½"

2'-8"

The 16th Essence Music Festival

• Organic Stage Sculpture + Projection Mapping

In 2010, The Essence Music Festival was held at the Louisiana Superdome and Ernest N. Morial Convention Center in New Orleans, L.A. featuring artists Janet Jackson, Mary J. Blige, LL Cool J, Alicia Keys, and Earth, Wind and Fire.

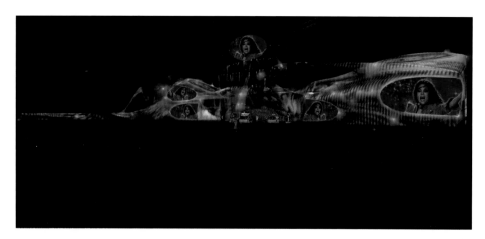

Production Designer: Stefan Beese, Re:Be Design

3D Designer: Seyavash Zohoori

Lighting Designer: John Clarke

Lighting Designer for Janet Jackson: Vince Foster

Producer: Rehage Entertainment Inc

Rigging: Steve Brown, Rhino Staging

Client: Essence Communications Inc.

The production and stage design by Stefan Beese of RE:BE Design exhibited an organic and fluid sculpture, as one large-scale projection screen by merging traditional, separate scenic and screen elements, which allowed for the variability of surface content and appearance.

The angled stage canopy masked the back of house production elements, such as the work deck and VIP area, which also maximized the visibility of video and performance content for both the floor and upper levels of the Superdome. The organic sculpture surface had been realised by using the 35,000 square yards of silver and white spandex, 12, 800 feet of nylon polyester thread, 9, 000 feet of rope and aircraft cables and 6, 000 feet of aluminum pipes, optimizing the fabulous video mapping effect.

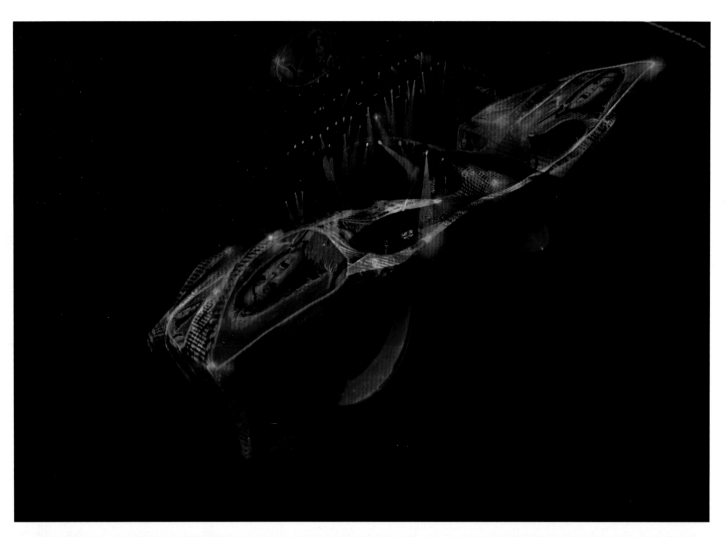

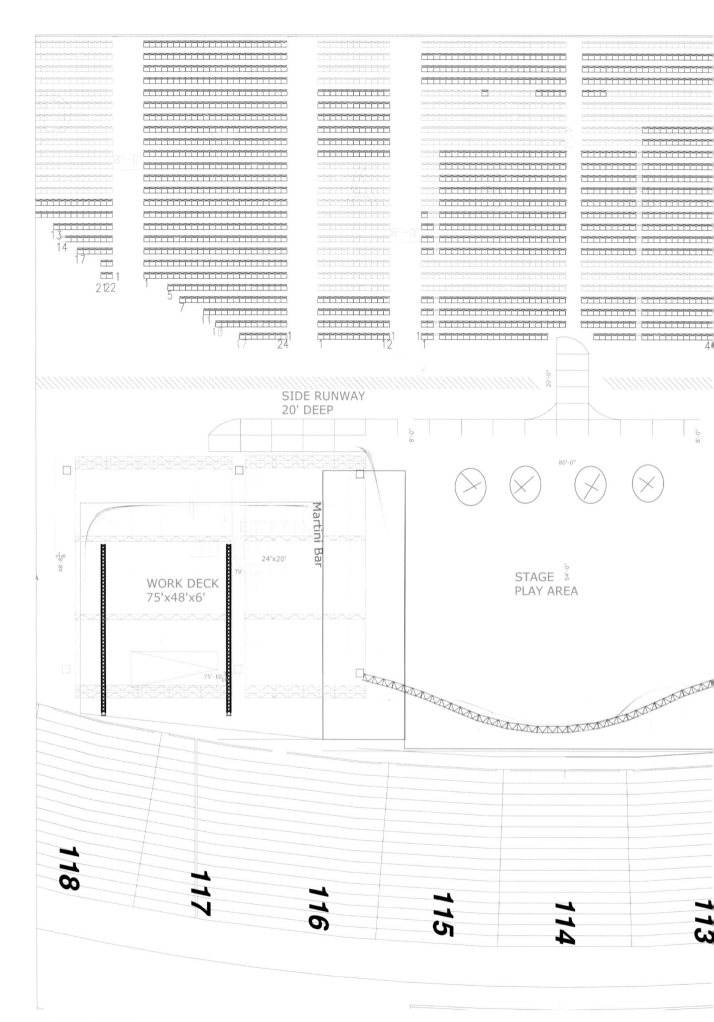

SIDE RUNWAY
20' DEEP

Martini Bar

24'x20'

WORK DECK
75'x48'x6'

TV

75'-10"

80'-0"

STAGE
PLAY AREA

118

117

116

115

114

113

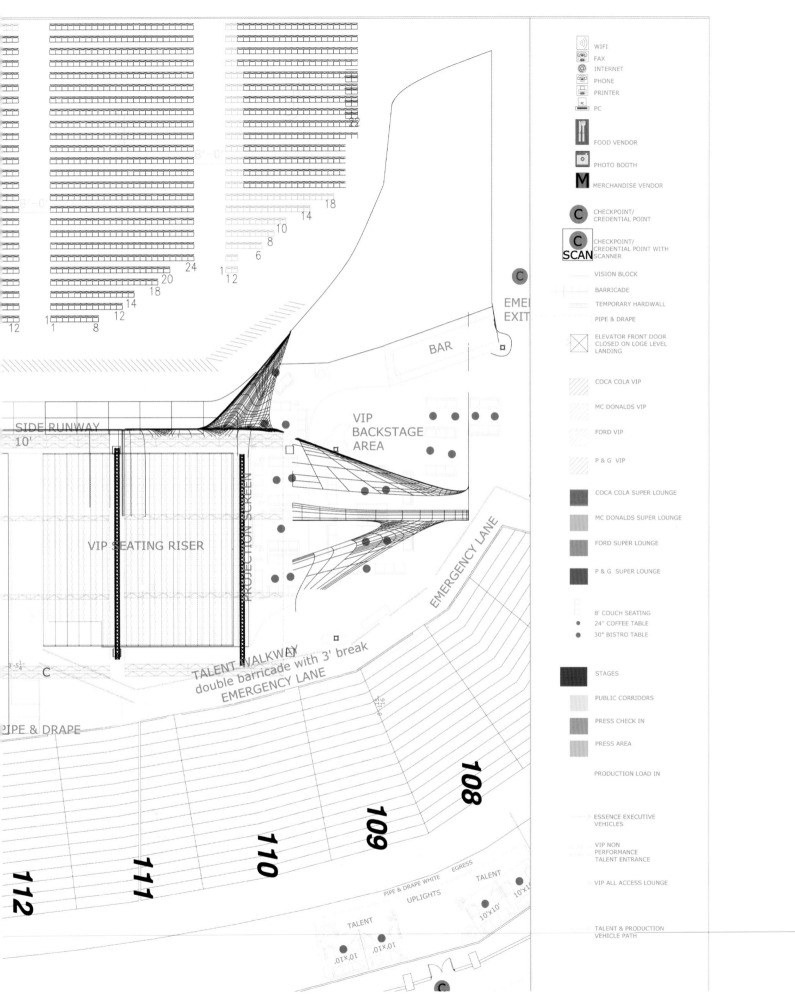

WIFI

FAX

INTERNET

PHONE

PRINTER

PC

FOOD VENDOR

PHOTO BOOTH

M MERCHANDISE VENDOR

C CHECKPOINT/
CREDENTIAL POINT

C
SCAN CHECKPOINT/
CREDENTIAL POINT WITH
SCANNER

VISION BLOCK

BARRICADE

TEMPORARY HARDWALL

PIPE & DRAPE

ELEVATOR FRONT DOOR
CLOSED ON LOGE LEVEL
LANDING

COCA COLA VIP

MC DONALDS VIP

FORD VIP

P & G VIP

COCA COLA SUPER LOUNGE

MC DONALDS SUPER LOUNGE

FORD SUPER LOUNGE

P & G SUPER LOUNGE

8' COUCH SEATING

24" COFFEE TABLE

30" BISTRO TABLE

STAGES

PUBLIC CORRIDORS

PRESS CHECK IN

PRESS AREA

PRODUCTION LOAD IN

ESSENCE EXECUTIVE
VEHICLES

VIP NON
PERFORMANCE
TALENT ENTRANCE

VIP ALL ACCESS LOUNGE

TALENT & PRODUCTION
VEHICLE PATH

SIDE RUNWAY
10'

VIP
BACKSTAGE
AREA

BAR

EMER
EXIT

VIP SEATING RISER

PROJECTION SCREEN

EMERGENCY LANE

TALENT WALKWAY
double barricade with 3' break
EMERGENCY LANE

PIPE & DRAPE

108

109

110

111

112

PIPE & DRAPE WHITE

EGRESS

TALENT

UPLIGHTS

10'X10'

10'X10'

TALENT

10'X10'

10'X10'

C

H2O Music Festival

• Side-screened main stage + Multi-functional towers

Univision Communications, Inc. is an American Spanish language media company. Designer Stefan Beese and his team at RE:BE Design completed the full production design for the inaugural H2O Music Festival in Dallas on June 9, 2012 and Los Angeles on August 25, 2012.

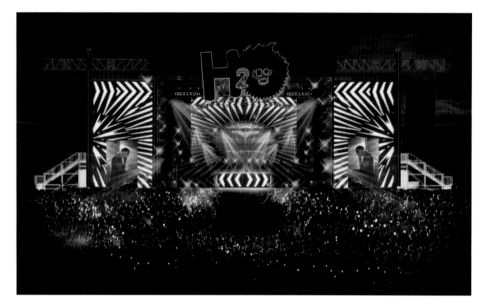

Production Designer: Stefan Beese, RE: BE Design

Visual Media Programmer: Matt Webb

System Designer: Cameron Yeary

Video Director: Stephen Bowels

Lighting Programmer: Nick Deel

Client: Univision Communications Inc.

The team worked with Univision Radio to build a festival identity that represented second generation Hispanics and established it as the premiere bilingual and multicultural musical experience in North America.

To achieve cohesiveness between the stage and the ground, Beese developed conceptual, Swiss Army Knife-like structures of tower shape that could accommodate multiple functions, used for branding of the festival promoter and sponsors, seating, cell-phone charging, shading, misting and lighting, which are by CNC technology perforated with logos on the aluminum panel cladding. These towers scattered on the site created a "cityscape" inside the Cotton Bowl, as an extension of L.A. skyline. With vertical screens and intelligent lighting within, the towers were visually connected with the main stage to make for a united, dynamic light show.

The fully digital stage featured two 50' x 30' Go vision Daktronics PST-12HD tiled by side-screens with special masks for floating image, keeping the performances dynamic and uniqueness to each artist. Not only did the vertical screens allow for a larger presence during close-ups, it also enforced the concept of "city of towers" presented on the festival ground.

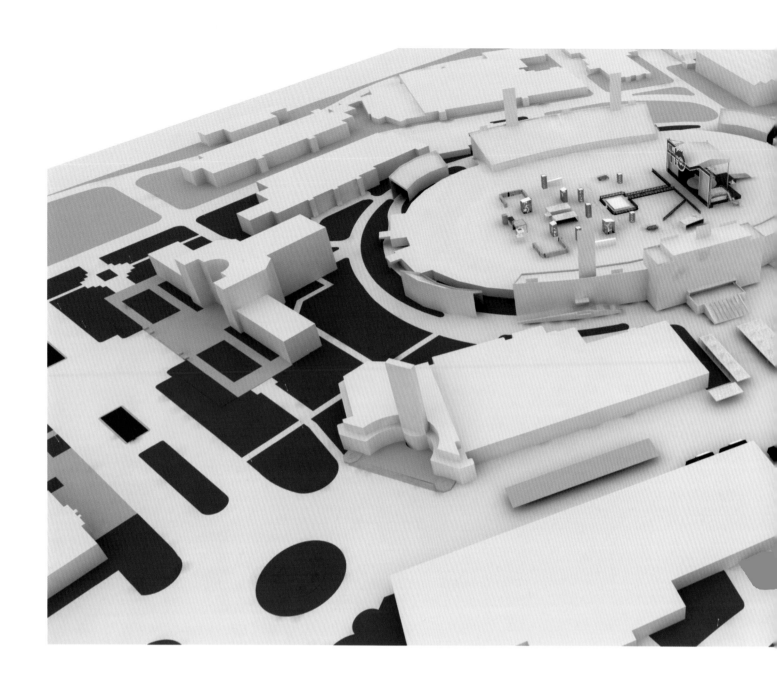

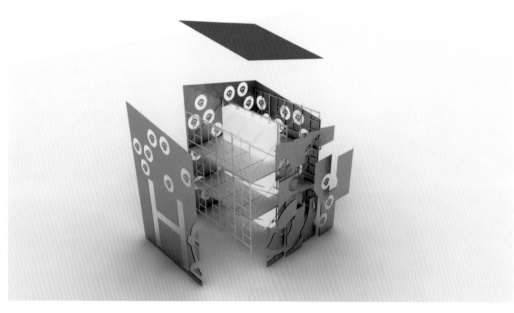

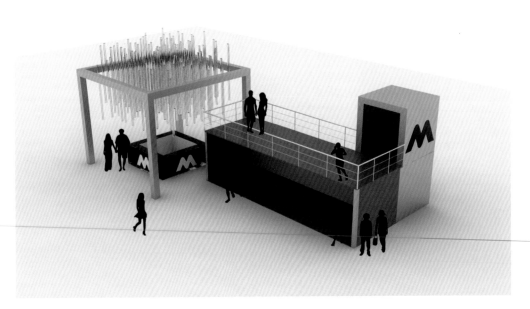

London Olympic Closing Ceremony

• A Union Flag Performance Stage

The 2012 Olympic Games was a major opportunity for stainless steel and a show of modern industry. £2.4 billion was spent only for the 30 venues, and more spent on infrastructure projects. The game had been organized by the Olympic Delivery Authority (ODA) and the London Organizing Committee of the Olympic and Paralympic Games.

Creative Director: Kim Gavin

Stage Designer: Es Devlin

Musical Director: David Arnold

Costume Designer: Michael Sharp

Lighting Designer: Patrick Woodroffe

Visual Artist: Damien Hirst

Video Designer: Luke Halls

Photo Credit: Jason Alden, Getty Images, NBC

The Olympic Closing Ceremony has a set-up time of just 12 hours without rehearsal in the Stadium and a global audience of around a billion... The design team had been advised not to be ambitious. Surely, they had just entirely ignored. Their main visual statement was a fragmented expression of the national flag, the Union Jack, redefined as an anarchic centrifugal explosion of painting by British pop artist Damien Hirst. It was a lavish affair, featuring 4,100 performers--3,500 volunteers and 380 schoolchildren from the six Olympic host boroughs. Some 20 British musicians with household names appeared, performing 30 pieces of famous British music.

The 11th Myer Spring-Summer Collections Launch

• *The Seashell Installation*

Myer is Australian's largest chain department stores, retailing a broad range of merchandise aiming at the high-end market. Myer's vision was to create original and creative environment for its fashion launches to show its own innovative approach of design. Myer Collections Launch Spring-Summer11 was held at the Eveleigh Carriageworks in Sydney in August 2010.

Production Designer: Rizer

Stage Designers: Chris Bosse, Tobias Wallisser, Alexander Rieck

Production Company: LAVA – Laboratory for Visionary Architecture

Creative Concept: Amanda Henderson, Gloss Creative

Architectural Co-creator: Chris Bosse, LAVA with Jarrod Lamshed

Manufacturing: Staging Rentals

Client: Myer Store

Photo Credit: Rocket Mattler

For the 11th Myer Collections Spring-Summer Launch, sand and seashells were the inspiration for this set designed by Chris Bosse from LAVA and Amanda Henderson from Gloss Creative.

The giant seashell structure was a sand-colored plywood installation with 18m length and 5m height. Digitally designed and CNC cut, it consisted of 2,000 sliced pieces, putting together just like a puzzle to imitate the geometry of a triton shell, strictly mathematical but of manifold manifestations. It was reflective of both the blonde colors of the season and the bleached beauty of the Australian beach. Models moved through the shell, then onto the catwalk. The installation reflected many themes, from sea goddesses at sunrise to sirens at sunset, embracing the diversified stage needs and featuring thirty Australian designers in the show.

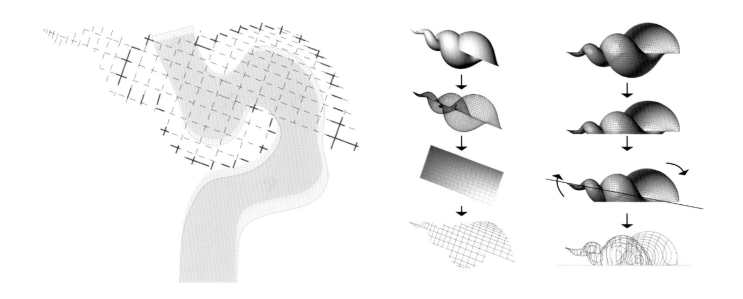

The 85th Oscars Academy Awards

• *Stage Lighting Sculpture*

Starting at 5:30pm, the 85th Academy Awards was held in the Dolby Theatre in Hollywood, LA. It is the first Oscar that was given the official name The Oscars in its promotion. The theme of this Oscar was about "music in the movies".

Producers: Neil Meron and Craig Zadan

Designer: Derek McLane

Photo Credit: A.M.P.A.S, Gloria Lamb

To create the stage, Tony-winning set designer Derek McLane, whose Broadway credits include set designs for 33 Variations, The Heiress, the soon-to-open Breakfast at Tiffany's and many award-winning projects, went back to the roots of theater. He was tasked with courage, reaching the state that no Academy Awards scenic designer has reached before.

McLane mentioned that the main inspiration came from an embellishment in his house—a wall installation featuring dozens of antique lamps in cubbyholes backed by iodizing mirrors. The installation on the stage was the half-moon shaped lighting sculpture that framed the gigantic stage of the Dolby Theatre at the Hollywood & Highland Center in Los Angeles. This installation stressed on making the ceremony a show for not only the television audience but also the ones sitting in Dolby. The antique feeling of the set also answered to the present theme of the event.

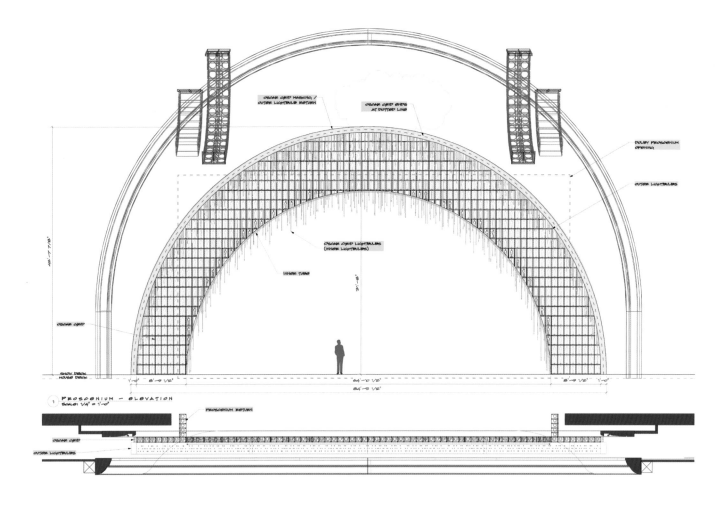

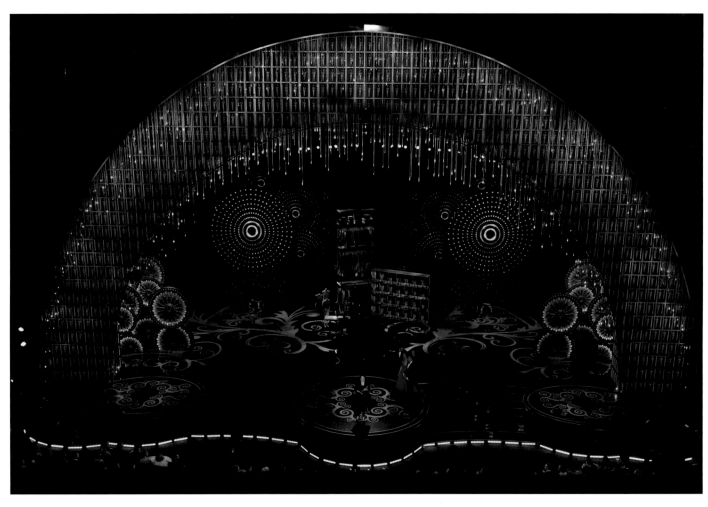

The Voice of Germany

• *The Voice of a Stage*

The Voice of Germany was premiered on 24 November 2011 on ProSieben and Sat.1. Based on the reality singing competition The Voice of Holland, it is part of an international series of The Voice. The German edition was produced by Talpa Media and Schwartzkopff TV Productions.

Production Designer: Florian Wieder

Art Director: Michaela Schmiele

Designer: Georg Boerner, Thomas Richter

Lighting Designer: Manuel da Costa

Assistant Lighting Designer: Michael Baganz

Client: ProSiebenSat.1 TV Deutschland GmbH

Photo Credit: The Voice of Germany

For the stage, designer Florian Wieder created three settings for three different phases of the contest, the Blind Auditions, the Battles, and the Live Show respectively. For the Blind Auditions, the main features are revolving chairs with buzzers, each of them was with a name sign and a monitoring box for perfect sound effect. Meanwhile, the stage in the center of the studio was shaped into a boxing ring surrounded by LED ropes, leading away by four catwalks at the corners, the space stressed by four large brackets, to form two parallel structures and impart a sense of solemnity and intensity.

In the Live Show part, the main stage was surrounded by a large band on both sides and was arranged rightly in front of the coaches. The background was large LED walls in a barcode appearance, and the large one in the middle was a dividable door for contestants' entry. Two LED catwalks directing to two small satellite stages were added to create an extra space for performance.

Lighting designer Manuel da Costa, one of Germany's leading television lighting designers, lit up the TVOG scene. He used about 300 moving lights to bring the stage set to life with inspiring lighting dynamics. "My task was to find a lighting concept that allowed me to the utmost creative flexibility, given the large number of songs to play. The stage had to be continuously transformed but with a uniform 'new light' shining each time. I had to put something special on the stage which was suitable for each song and each artist. We wanted to make the visual highlights stand out, without overburdening the set and running the risk of 'smothering'," explained da Costa.

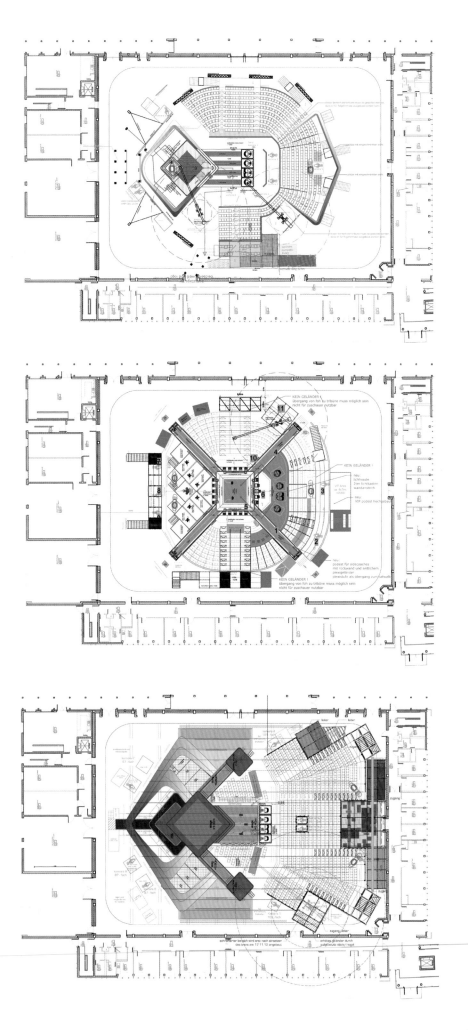

The Power of Creation

• Decorated Arches + Lightening Effect

Dom Pérignon is a brand of vintage Champagne produced by the Champagne house Moët & Chandon and serves as the house's prestige product. The concert and gala dinner entitled The Power of Creation by Champagne house Dom Pérignon was taken place at Union Church, Shanghai.

Design Company: Han's Studio

Creative Director / Art Director: Lixun Han

Client: Dom Pérignon

The event brought two talented artists together: Alexandre Desplat, a Golden Globe-winning film-score composer, and the internationally acclaimed pianist Lang Lang. Inspired by the complex nature of Dom Perignon champagne, Desplat composed three original movements, which were brought to life by Lang Lang's deft performance under the roof of the iconic Union Church in Shanghai. Designer Lixun Han drew inspiration from the power of creation and the unique characteristics of Dom Pérignon to create an intimate and inspiring setting enriched by atmospheric light design. The seamless collaboration resulted in a multi-sensory event to respond to the theme—The Power of Creation.

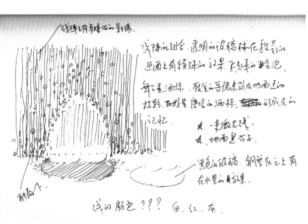

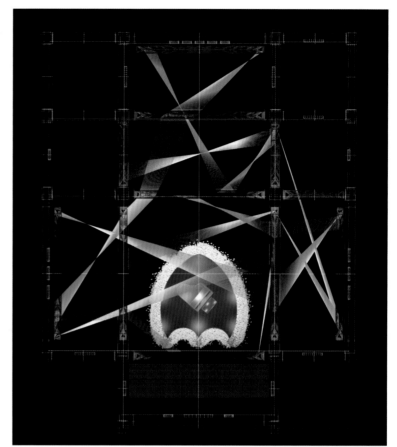

The 65th Bregenz Festival

• *Marat Sculpture*

The Bregenz Festival is a performing arts festival which is held every July and August in Bregenz, Austria since 1946. A combination of variables included the breathtaking natural surroundings, impressive stage setting, and transition through various daylight-to-dusk panoramic and background settings leaving you daydreaming with unforgettable memories.

Stage Designer: Jonannes Leaacker

Artist: Karl Forster, Simon Wimmer

The lake stage of 2011 and 2012 were endowed with the background of the French Revolution, the opera André Chénier by Italian composer Umberto Giordano. The end version of the stage design was a 24-meter-high Marat-sculpture, which was the figure from "The Death of Marat", a 1793 painting in the neoclassic style by Jacques-Louis David. Many other elements of the stage design included a gold mirror, an old book or a letter held in the hands of Marat. The 19-meter-wide and 7-meter-high gold mirror played a role not only as decoration but also as a venue for extras and stuntmen.

Bregenz Festival: Tosca

• *The Giant Eye*

This is another out-of-the-world stage designed for the Bregenz Festival. The over-sized eye successfully captured the attentions of millions of people globally, making the stage design a timeless creation.

Puccini's Tosca on the lake-stage of Bregenz Festival was a spectacular stage setting that cheered the audience up in the summer of 2007 and 2008. The lake provided a brilliant backdrop for the surrealist stage setting– a stage dominated by a giant eye, changing throughout the opera to become, at times, a screen where the face of Tosca was superimposed, an opening door to reveal a chorus of bishops, priests and other church officials, an execution platform for the unfortunate Cavaradossi and finally, the edge from which he falls. The giant eye lighted up the whole stage and gave an electrifying performance to the audience.

Director: Philipp Himmelmann

Stager Designer: Johannes Leiacker

Artist: Benno Hagleitner

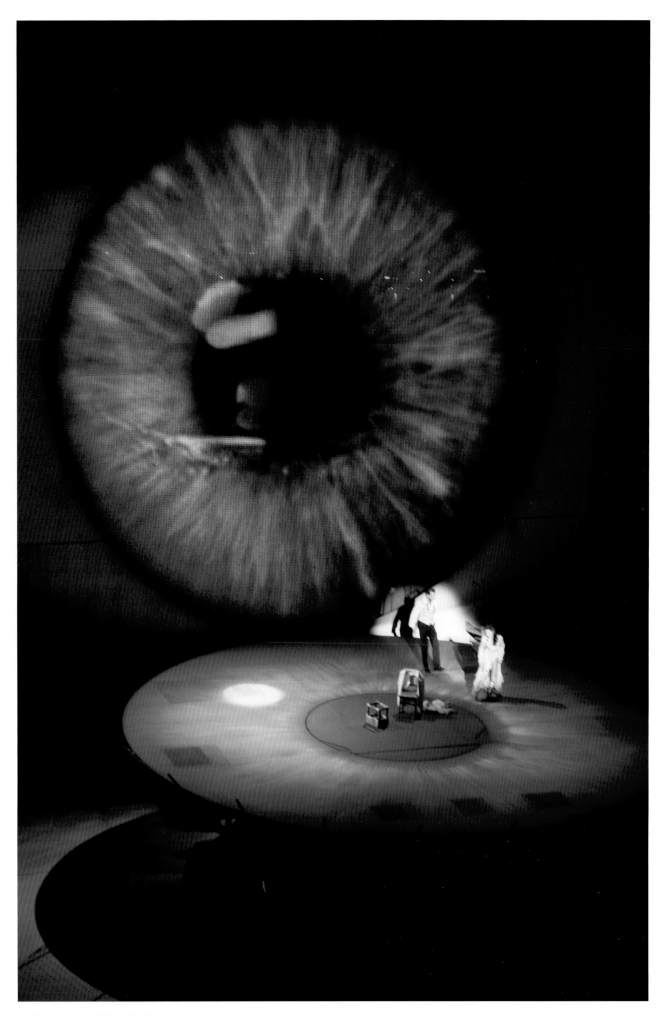

MTV Australian Music Awards

• Hight-weight Fabric

LAVA designed the "MTV" installation specifically for the MTV Awards 2009. Suspended in the Sydney Convention Centre and spanning from 35m to 24m, the sculpture provided an intense visual environment for the global TV show.

Design: Laboratory for Visionary Architecture

Client: MTV Australia

Location: Sydney, Australia

Realized in lightweight fabric, this MTV Stage was a digital design derived from nature and used the latest digital fabrication and engineering techniques to create more with less. The installation was fastly tracked to meet the MTV Awards Ceremony 2009 broadcasting to millions of audience around the globe.

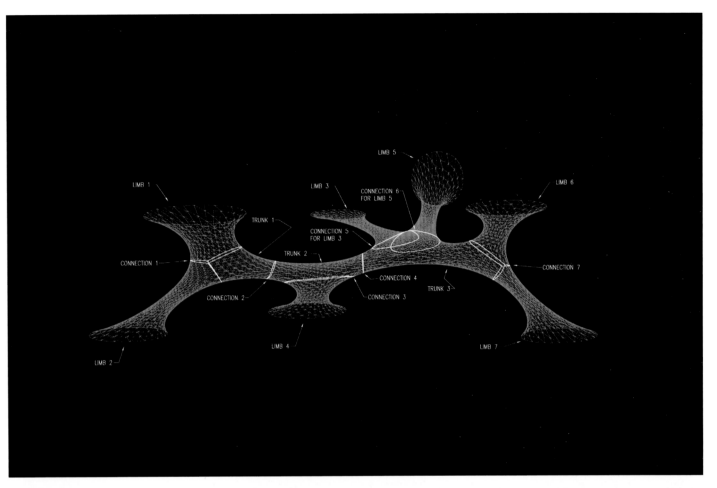

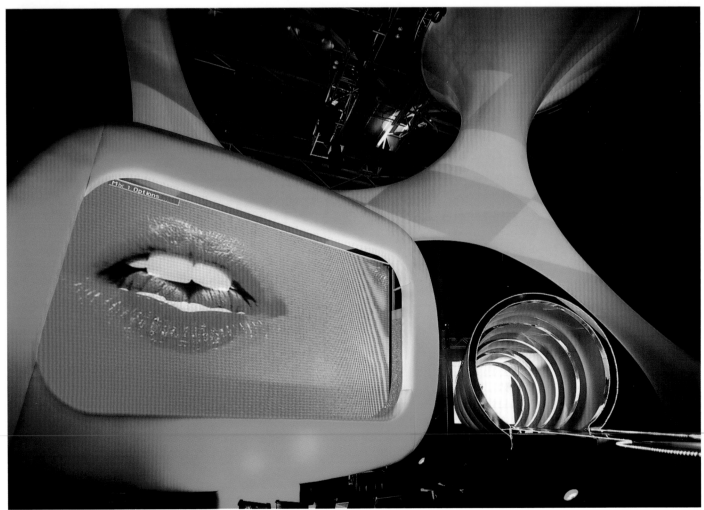

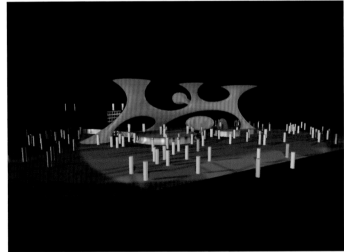

The 81st Annual Academy Awards

• *Swarovski Crystal Curtain*

David Rockwell designed the sets for the world-renowned ceremony, the 81st Annual Academy Awards. As the first architect designing the sets, Rockwell used his extensive background in crafting immersive three-dimensional environments to create a fresh look for the Oscars.

Design Company: Rockwell Group

Client: Academy of Motion Picture Arts and Sciences

Location: Hollywood, USA

Rockwell developed sets to evoke an elegant party instead of a formal performance atmosphere. The innovative and glamorous technologies and designs were combined with an emphasis on spectacle and community. In a nod to the high-profile fashion associated with this event, the designer created a new proscenium and a curtain comprised of approximately 100,000 Swarovski Crystals in a variety of shapes and sizes. The sparkle and magic of the curtain paved the way for the unexpected elements of the design.

The 82nd Annual Academy Awards

• *Swarovski Crystal Curtain*

In 2010 David Rockwell designed the sets for the world-renowned Academy Awards ceremony for the second year in a row. Working with Oscar telecast producers Adam Shankman and Bill Mechanic, Rockwell built and expanded on many of the design innovations which just had been introduced last year.

Design Company: Rockwell Group

Client: Academy of Motion Picture Arts and Sciences

Location: Hollywood, USA

The white template of the stage, combined with new integrated LED and projected imagery, created a constant play of imagery, light and movement. Added into these effects were three circular platforms acting as moving turntables on stage with multiple levels for a variety of focal points, camera setups and presentation locations. Rockwell reprised one of the most dazzling elements of last design–the Swarovski Crystal curtain. The designer also kept the new orchestra seating structure in order to retain the intimacy that was achieved in the show in the previous year.

✴ ✴ ✴

THEATERS

Theater is an art with the audio-visual
media. Therefore, the stage design
for theater is an art of modeling
which is with the regulation of plastic
arts, such as painting and sculpture.
Furthermore, design for theatrical
stages must take movements or
actions of the actors into account.
The designs for action, models,
spaces and images are the primary
missions of the stage design for
theaters. As the development of
the art, the aesthetic requirement of
audiences is increasing. If the stage
design for theater stays with traditions
without innovation, it cannot fulfill
ever more demanding taste of the
audiences. At presence and in the
future, the current trend of the stage
design for theaters is diversified and
is devoted to delivering not only the
drama itself for the audiences, but
also visual metaphors hidden in the
drama.

Spider Man: Turn off the Dark

• Tilting proscenium + Pop-up Techniques

The musical is based on Spider-Man comics created by Stan Lee and Steve Ditko, its namesake film in 2002 and the Greek myth of Arachne. The story spins around the origin of the character, his romance with Mary Jane and his battles with the evil Green Goblin.

Production Director: Julie Taymor, Philip William McKinley

Stage Design & Art Installations: George Tsypin

Costume Designer: Eiko Ishioka

Lighting Designer: Donald Holder

Choreographer: Daniel Ezralow

Music Composer: Bono, The Edge

Construction Company: PRG Scenic Technologies

The first hard nut to be cracked for Stage designer George Tsypin in designing the scene for Spider-Man: Turn Off the Dark was about how to achieve a similar elliptical thrill without Hollywood's green screens and special effects but still let the iconic hero swing from the comic pages to towering buildings in a spectacular fashion. He rose to the challenge by a pop-up solution and by making everything moving.

The show included stunts of high-tech, such as actors swinging between "webs" and several aerial combat scenes. "The entire environment we've created is kinetic and dynamic," Tsypin said, "but you also see New York from a different perspective, as if you were able to jump buildings and to fly over Manhattan. It's a whole different experience. And New York is, of course, as important a chapter in this story as Spider-Man himself."

He firstly began a period of intensive experimentation with a team of illustrators to learn pop-up techniques, for which "there's no computer program and professional pop-up illustrators weren't very helpful, as what we were doing was so different." No one thought it could be done, until lightweight and durable carbon fiber was adopted as the primary set material.

Graphically, New York predominated in the show. "But there's a certain style for the architectures in the comic books, which is usually in the background and very dry, not expressive." Then Tsypin decided to set the scenery in black and white, yet alive with color lightly. The huge skyscrapers looked like cardboard cutouts but in fact were sophisticated panels with LED lights and many layers of materials. Lighting designer Don Holder lighted the show from the front, back and inside with colors.

At the same time the stage designer kept the staff of PRG Scenic Technologies busy with innovations. "The proscenium was the most difficult thing for the shop to create," he continued, "It's not just about the light box element, but also that it should be permeable for the sound and packed with pop-up pieces like a giant Spider-Man and Green Goblin." The entire proscenium was tilting—one panel went one way, a second goes another.

An audience favorite in Act I was "Bouncing Off the Walls," where the empowered Peter Parker did that in his home. "That's another piece taking a long time," "In the beginning, the room was supposed to rotate, and then it evolved into something more puppet-like. Puppeteers operate the very light walls, which are built of carbon fiber and fabric - the idea is a 3D trampoline made of material that's very soft. It adds to the concept of a world in motion."

"Audiences in the balcony, the best place to watch the entire breadth of the show, would see Spider-Man's landing all but on their laps when he flies." Tsypin Says, "I want him to walk sideways around the balcony, but there's too many equipments there. Figuring out where to place the landing platforms was one of those decisions that were involved the totality of the theatre. The thing about this show is there's no wall between the stage and the house. We broke it to give the audience an incredible experience."

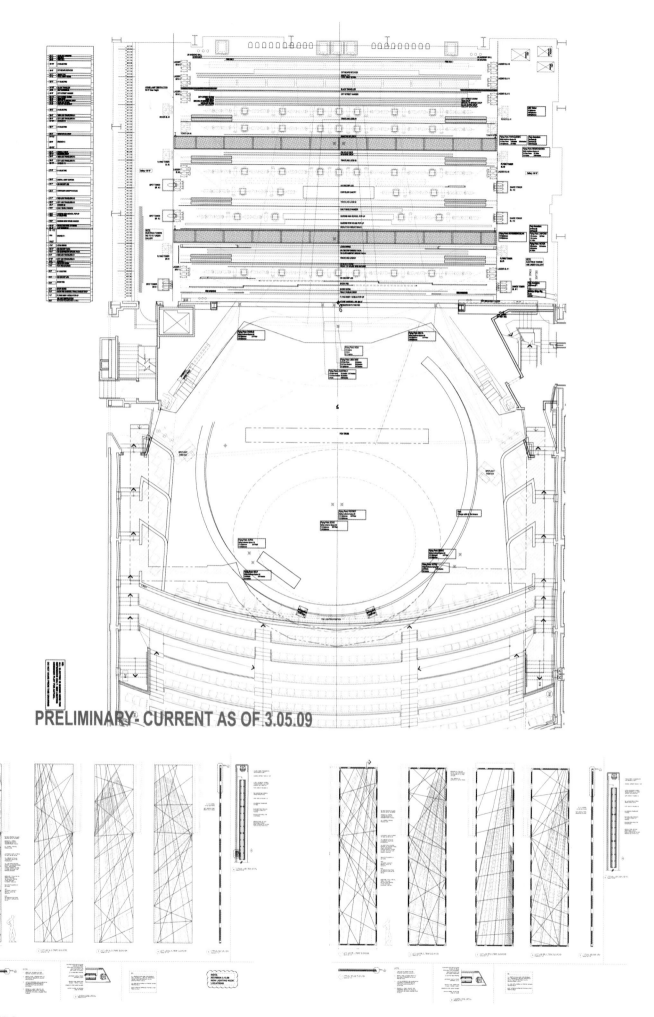

PRELIMINARY - CURRENT AS OF 3.05.09

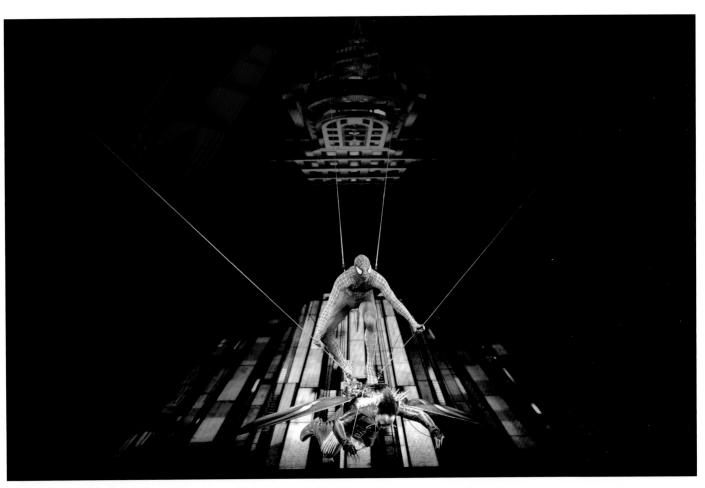

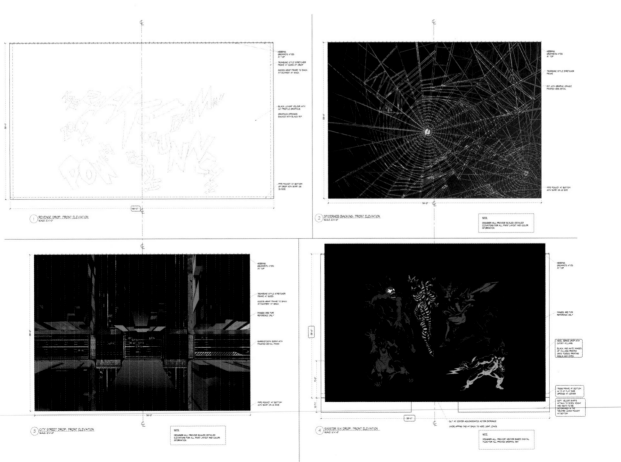

Face to Face with George Tsypin

From your designs, like the stages of 1999 MTV Awards, Flying Dutchman, the Mariinsky Ring in Cardiff and many more, we can see traces of sculpture, either in the form of video projection or stage structure, characterized by overwhelming line work and clear-cut shapes. Have you been aware of this aspect of your stage works or have you consciously made use of your sculpture experience? In what way do you think it has shaped you as a set designer?

Originally I was trained to be an architect in Moscow and in many ways it has made me a designer. I am still very inspired by the things I learned there. When I design for the theater, the overriding goal is to create an exciting space. The objects and built forms are created in order to shape that space. The lines, surfaces and the edges are there to form dramatic emptiness. They are also there in order to transform that space. Unlike architectural design, creating live shows is an ability to see the space and objects in motion, to be able to imagine an event and the transformation that resonates with either the music, or the story. Usually the creative process boils down to conceiving that kinetic composition that incorporates the elements of architecture, sculpture and lighting at the same time.

You have told us that your team had had a hard time experimenting with pop-up techniques in the Spiderman project, but would you please tell us more on that? For example, where you had started, what difficulties had you run into, how the problem got solved and how the resulting structures were combined with patterns and lighting effect ?

When I started working on Spiderman I immediately realized that I needed to find 3D equivalent to the graphic way of telling the story in the comic books. I had to find a unique theatrical language that captures the raw power of graphic novels. It had to be sculptural, dynamic and graphic at the same time. Pop-up books came to my mind. The beauty of pop-up books is that they have this dramatic quality: seemingly out of nothing, out of flat page of the book a full 3D world emerges. That transformation is always delightfully surprising and completely unexpected.

This early idea was also very important on very practical level: it allowed to "pack" the sets flat in a very compact way. The biggest problem of Broadway theaters is that they have no off-stage space. Broadway stages are very cramped and one has to be highly inventive in order to fit all the sets and a multitude of different looks required by the way you tell the story in Broadway musical. However, on the other hand it was also a very impractical idea because paper pop-ups in the book are virtually impossible to translate into a large scale. Paper is a unique, almost magic material – it is soft and hard at the same time, flexible, yet pliable. There is no equivalent to paper in large scale. The physics just don't work.

It took many months of experiments and building of countless samples to find a way to approaching this. We used super light high-tech materials, very advanced mechanics and sometime old fashioned theatrical tricks and illusion to realize large scale pop-ups. I believe we were the first ones to do this.

Based on your description, it looks like that this project is not only about "designing" but also about "inventing" – to create something there isn't. So we believe you must have learned a lot from the whole experience and what would you like to share with the reader, especially to fellow stage designers?

The most difficult thing about designing for a theater is that you always have to start from scratch. You cannot use old and tried technique. Theater has to astonish. You as a designer have to amaze and surprise people. It is almost a superhuman effort to every time invent something new. The whole process is akin to walking in the dark, you don't know where you going, you lose the purpose and direction, but you have to keep going. When you get completely panic, desperate and hopeless – the miracle happens. All of a sudden, you know exactly what to do.

Abundance

• Frontier Adventures

Written by the Pulitzer Prize-winning author Beth Henley, this wickedly funny and deeply touching play follows the adventures of Bess and Macon, two mail-order brides on their twenty-five year journey across the American frontier. Outrageous catastrophes, a kidnapping, and bad marriages test their lifelong friendship.

Director: Jenn Thompson

Stage Designer: Wilson Chin

Lighting Designer: Philip S. Rosenberg

Costume Designer: Tracy Christensen

Sound Designer: Toby Jaguar Algya

Client: Hartford Stage

Photo Credit: T. Charles Erickson

This play Abundance was set against the American frontier in the late 1800's. Scenic designer Wilson Chin wanted to capture the heat, loneliness and expansive landscape of that time and place by using raw and contemporary materials. So the deck was made of unpainted OSB chipboard, which is a common kind of building material, while the backdrop was made out of raw burlap that has been layered, textured and frayed to look like a mountain range.

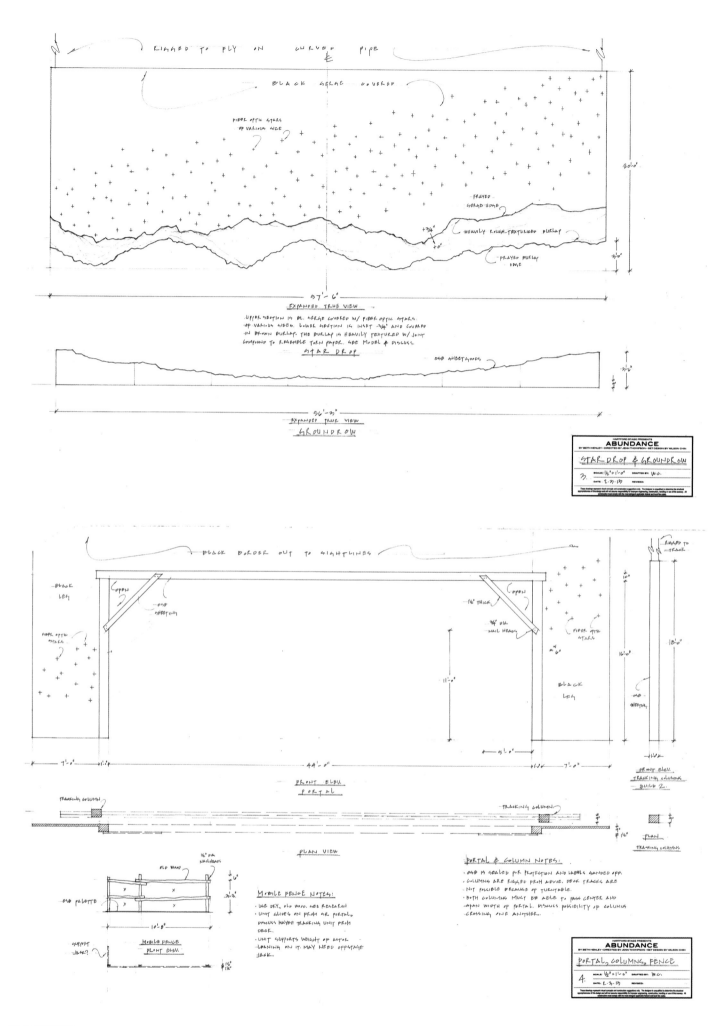

RIGGED TO FLY ON CURVED ₵ PIPE

BLACK SCRAG COVERED

FIBER OPTIC STARS
OF VARIOUS SIZE

FRAYED
SCRAG EDGE

HEAVILY ROUGH TEXTURED BURLAP

+3/4"
+0"

FRAYED BURLAP
EDGE

20'-0"

3'-0"

37'-6"

EXPANDED TRUE VIEW

UPPER SECTION IS BL. SCRAG COVERED W/ FIBER OPTIC STARS
OF VARIOUS SIZES. LOWER SECTION IS INSET 3/4" AND COVERED
IN BROWN BURLAP. THE BURLAP IS HEAVILY TEXTURED W/ JOINT
COMPOUND TO RESEMBLE TORN PAPER. SEE MODEL & DISCUSS.

STAR DROP

OSB SHEETGOODS

2'-6"

56'-3"

EXPANDED TRUE VIEW

GROUNDROW

HARTFORD STAGE PRESENTS
ABUNDANCE
BY BETH HENLEY • DIRECTED BY JENN THOMPSON • SET DESIGN BY WILSON CHIN

STAR DROP & GROUNDROW

3. SCALE: 1/2"=1'-0"   DRAFTED BY: W.C.
    DATE: 2.27.17   REVISED:

BLACK BORDER OUT TO SIGHTLINES

RIGGED TO
TRACK

BLACK
LEG

OPEN

OSB
SHEETING

FIBER OPTIC
STARS

10'-0"

OPEN

1 1/2" THICK

3/4" DIA.
NAIL HEADS

FIBER OPTIC
STARS

6'-6"

16'-0"

18'-0"

11'-0"

BLACK
LEG

OSB
SHEETING

7'-0"

1'-6"

44'-0"

5'-0"

7'-0"

1'-6"

FRONT ELEV.
PORTAL

FRONT ELEV.
TRACKING COLUMNS
BUILD 2.

TRACKING COLUMN

TRACKING COLUMN

1 1/2"

1 1/2"

PLAN
TRACKING COLUMNS

PLAN VIEW

OLD WOOD

1/2" DIA
NAILHEADS

6"

2'-0"

OSB PALETTE

SUPPORT
JACK?

10'-0"

MOBILE FENCE
FRONT ELEV.

1 1/2"
1 1/2"

MOBILE FENCE NOTES:
• USE DRY, OLD WOOD. OBS RESEARCH
• UNIT GLIDES ON BEAM OR PORTAL.
  DISCUSS MAYBE TRACKING UNIT FROM
  DECK.
• UNIT SUPPORTS WEIGHT OF ACTOR
  LEANING ON IT. MAY NEED OFFSTAGE
  JACK.

PORTAL & COLUMN NOTES:
• OSB IS SEALED FOR PROJECTION AND LABELS SANDED OFF.
• COLUMNS ARE RIGGED FROM ABOVE. DECK TRACKS ARE
  NOT POSSIBLE BECAUSE OF TURNTABLE.
• BOTH COLUMNS MUST BE ABLE TO PASS CENTER AND
  SPAN WIDTH OF PORTAL. DISCUSS POSSIBILITY OF COLUMNS
  CROSSING ONE ANOTHER.

HARTFORD STAGE PRESENTS
ABUNDANCE
BY BETH HENLEY • DIRECTED BY JENN THOMPSON • SET DESIGN BY WILSON CHIN

PORTAL, COLUMNS, FENCE

4. SCALE: 1/2"=1'-0"   DRAFTED BY: W.C.
    DATE: 2.3.17   REVISED:

Anna Christie

• A Dark Romance + Water-related Scenes

Anna Christie is a gripping play of the relationship between an old sailor and the daughter he hasn't seen in 15 years. Their new bond becomes strained when she falls in love with a young man whose seafaring life isn't what her father wants for her. When Anna reveals to both men her shameful secret, they came to understand the harsh reality of her past and show her compassion, love and forgiveness. This poetic masterpiece won Eugene O'Neill his second Pulitzer Prize.

Directors: Daniel Goldstein, The Old Globe, CA

Stage Designer: Wilson Chin

Lighting Designer: Austin R. Smith

Costume Designer: Denitsa Bliznakova

Sound Designer: Paul Peterson

Original Music: Chris Miller

Client: The Old Globe

Scenic designer Wilson Chin wanted to use raw materials to tell this dark and gritty romance. Set at the New York harbor, Wilson Chin used hemp ropes to delineate space, rusted metal as deck surface, muddy plastic sheeting above as ceiling and large heavy wood pylons to surround the stage. As a final touch, he flooded the stage with fog for a moment set on the water, using a rectangular metal grating on the deck to control where the fog went.

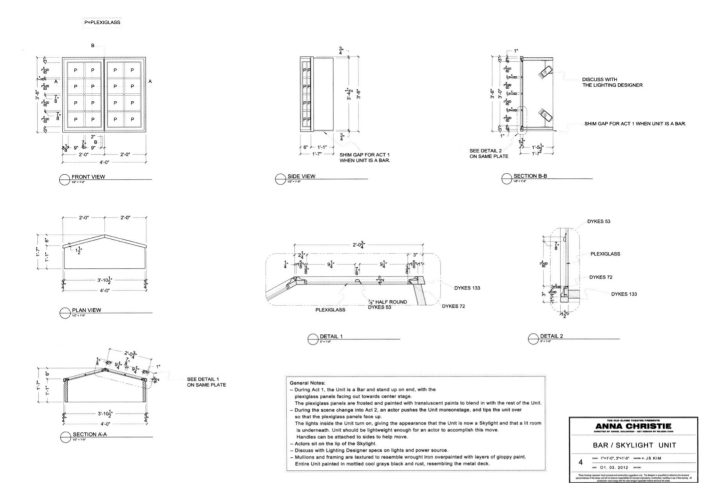

P=PLEXIGLASS

FRONT VIEW
1/2" = 1'-0"

SIDE VIEW
1/2" = 1'-0"

SHIM GAP FOR ACT 1
WHEN UNIT IS A BAR.

SECTION B-B
1/2" = 1'-0"

DISCUSS WITH
THE LIGHTING DESIGNER

SHIM GAP FOR ACT 1 WHEN UNIT IS A BAR.

SEE DETAIL 2
ON SAME PLATE

PLAN VIEW
1/2" = 1'-0"

DETAIL 1
3" = 1'-0"

7/8" HALF ROUND
DYKES 53

PLEXIGLASS

DYKES 133

DYKES 72

DETAIL 2
3" = 1'-0"

DYKES 53

PLEXIGLASS

DYKES 72

DYKES 133

SECTION A-A
1/2" = 1'-0"

SEE DETAIL 1
ON SAME PLATE

General Notes:
– During Act 1, the Unit is a Bar and stand up on end, with the
 plexiglass panels facing out towards center stage.
 The plexiglass panels are frosted and painted with transluscent paints to blend in with the rest of the Unit.
– During the scene change into Act 2, an actor pushes the Unit moreonstage, and tips the unit over
 so that the plexiglass panels face up.
 The lights inside the Unit turn on, giving the appearance that the Unit is now a Skylight and that a lit room
 is underneath. Unit should be lightweight enough for an actor to accomplish this move.
 Handles can be attached to sides to help move.
– Actors sit on the lip of the Skylight.
– Discuss with Lighting Designer specs on lights and power source.
– Mullions and framing are textured to resemble wrought iron overpainted with layers of gloppy paint.
 Entire Unit painted in mottled cool grays black and rust, resembling the metal deck.

THE OLD GLOBE THEATRE PRESENTS
ANNA CHRISTIE
DIRECTED BY DANIEL GOLDSTEIN · SET DESIGN BY WILSON CHIN

BAR / SKYLIGHT UNIT

4 SCALE: 1"=1'-0", 3"=1'-0" DRAWN BY: JS KIM
DATE: 01. 03. 2012 REVISION:

These drawings represent visual concepts and construction suggestions only. The designer is unqualified to determine the structural appropriateness of this design and will not assume responsibility for improper engineering, construction, handling or use of this scenery. All construction must comply with the most stringent applicable federal and local fire codes.

ANTIGONE, ISRAEL

• *Greek Tragedy Restaged + Long Table Setting*

Antigone is a tragedy by Sophocles written in or before 441 BC, as one of the most well-known Three Theban plays. It raises political issues relevant to almost any modern society. In Israel, due to its special circumstance (the second Lebanon-Israel war 2006), it created a link to the reality around immediately in the audience's mind even without actors dressed in Israeli uniforms.

Director: Hanan Snir

Designer: Roni Toren

Costumes designer: Ofra Confino

Lighting designer: Felice Ross

Due to the special timing of the design (2006), the artistic-team was debating whether the production should reflect the events going outside the theatre in any way. However, the production was basically dealing with reflections on the basic conflict between individual morals and the society rather than "a" war or country.

The design was faced with a known problem in modern productions for Greek dramas: what to be done with the chorus. The answer was given by arranging a large table, crossing the full length of the stage. The chorus, a group of war veterans (elderly respectable actors) were sitting around the table serving as a jury in an imaginary court. The events were brought in front of the court to be evaluated and concluded by a line written behind, up on the backdrop: "Great words of boasting bring great punishment."

Batman Live, World Arena Tour

• *3D Pop-up Installation + Projection Mapping*

Batman Live is a visually stunning production completed with a brand new original storyline. The live show featured Batman, the trusty counterpart Robin, the tireless butler Alfred and a host of other favorite Batman characters, including the villains such as The Joker, The Riddler, Catwoman and The Penguin. The story would take place in several settings from the famed DC Comics stories, including Gotham City, Wayne Manor, the Batcave and Arkham Asylum.

Creative Director: Anthony Van Laast

Production Designer: Es Devlin

Executive Producer: Nick Grace

Video Designer: Luke Halls / Sam Pattinson

Lighting Designer: Patrick Woodroffe

Technical Design Company: Tait Towers

Costume Designer: Jack Galloway

Music Composer: James Brett

Sound Designer: Simon Baker

By borrowing techniques from opera and animation production, designers created a 3D pop art environment on the arena, by a close understanding of the story of Bruce Wayne, the Batman, his struggles, and fight for justice, with state-of-the-art visuals and illusions. It took the design team eight weeks to make this miniature Gotham City, home of the hero.

Lighting designer Patrick Woodroffe put his professional skills into the darkened streets of the city. "Where a single three-quarter light spotted on an actor who had a dramatic monologue might mean something to 1,000 people, it doesn't make an impression on 15,000 in an arena. You have to find a different way to tell that part of the story without losing the intimacy and the subtlety of the moment," he explained.

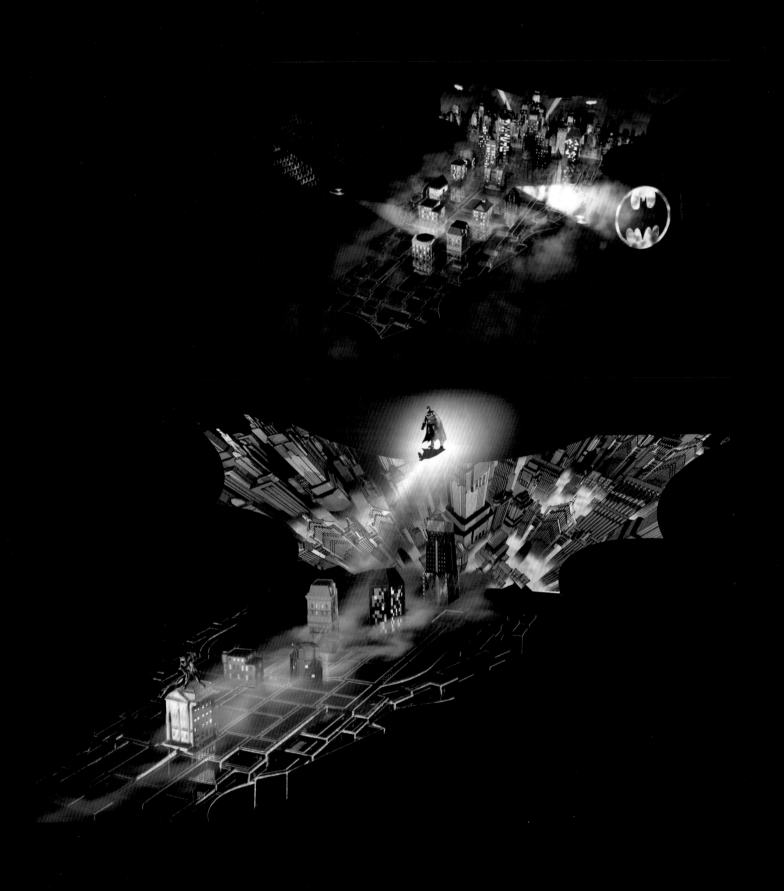

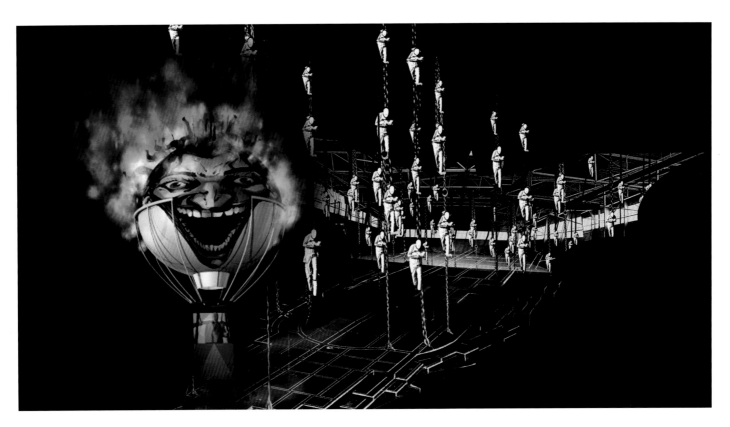

A mixture of circus-style stunts and industry-leading technology, video animation and special effects were supplied to bring the hero's story into life. To support the team's ideas, Tait Towers provided over 20 different technical elements, which were developed specifically for the set.

As the focus of the production, the center stage accumulated some complex elements including prop lifts, circular lifts, video integration and a pantographic staircase. It was supported by a Tait proprietary system which magnetically located the decks. The company also had set up parts in different sections of the arena floors, which allowed the aerial mother grid and stage to work simultaneously. Once the grid has been lifted, each stage section can be rolled into the place aligned with total accuracy and speed.

An interesting part of the Batman Live set-up is how it truly incorporated video into the live action story. Not only were the screens part of the scenery (bat-shaped screen), but they provided a comic strip cartoon backdrop, an element to separate this show from traditional theatre.

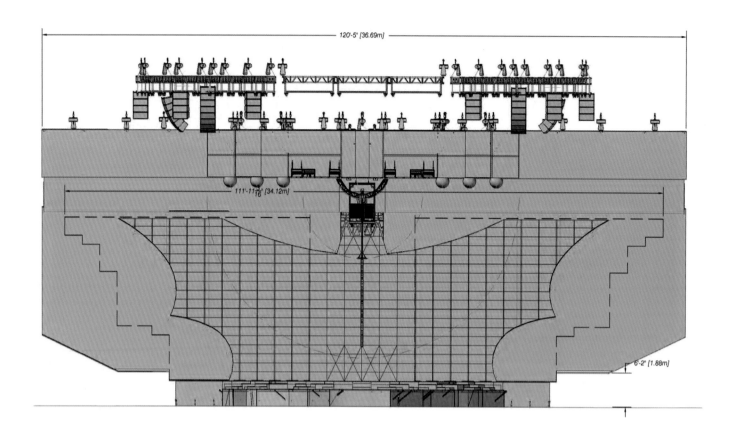

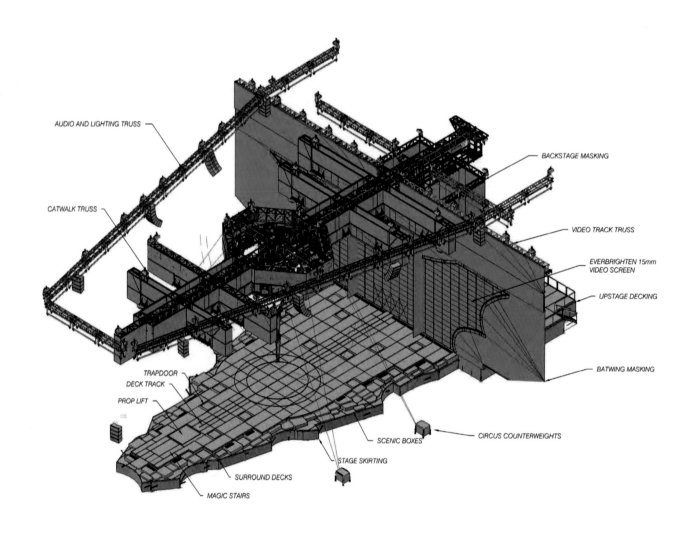

AUDIO AND LIGHTING TRUSS

BACKSTAGE MASKING

CATWALK TRUSS

VIDEO TRACK TRUSS

EVERBRIGHTEN 15mm
VIDEO SCREEN

UPSTAGE DECKING

TRAPDOOR

DECK TRACK

PROP LIFT

BATWING MASKING

SCENIC BOXES

CIRCUS COUNTERWEIGHTS

STAGE SKIRTING

SURROUND DECKS

MAGIC STAIRS

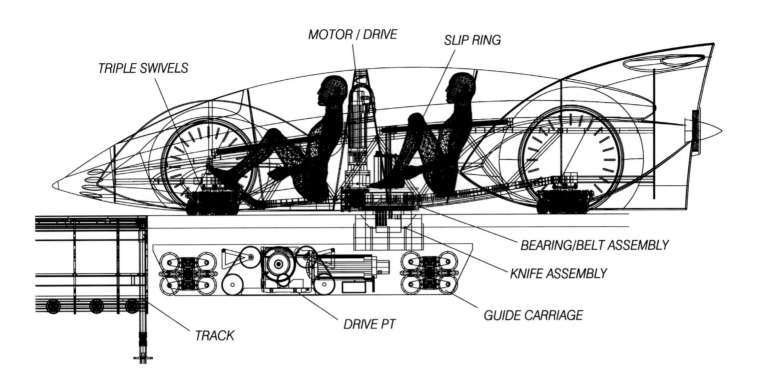

TRIPLE SWIVELS

MOTOR / DRIVE

SLIP RING

BEARING/BELT ASSEMBLY

KNIFE ASSEMBLY

GUIDE CARRIAGE

DRIVE PT

TRACK

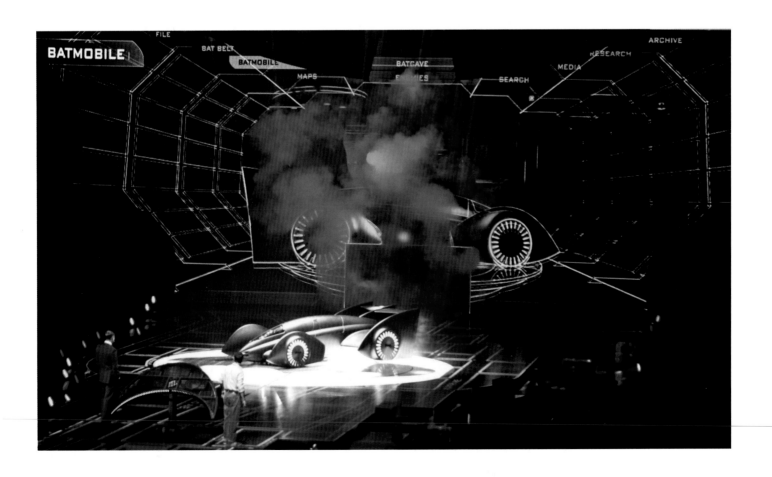

BATMOBILE

FILE

BAT BELT

BATMOBILE

MAPS

BATCAVE

SEARCH

MEDIA

RESEARCH

ARCHIVE

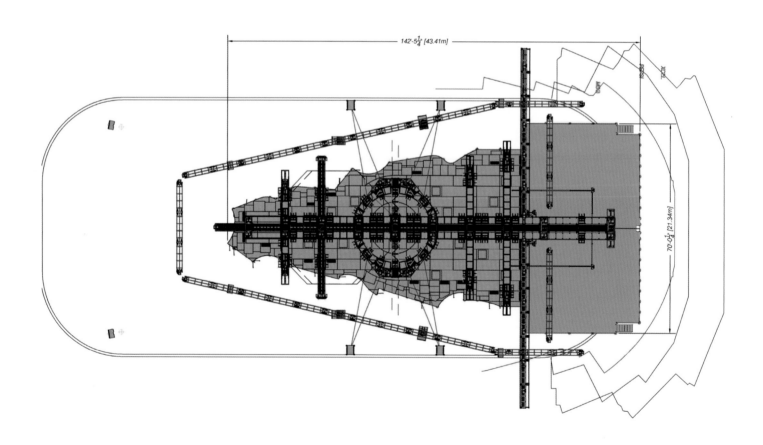

142-5¼ [43.41m]

70-0¼ [21.34m]

CABARET, ISRAEL

• Sliding Walls + Projection Mapping

Cabaret was based on John Van Druten's 1951 play "I Am a Camera", which in turn was adapted from the novel "Goodbye to Berlin" by Christopher Isherwood. Set in 1931, Berlin where Nazis were rising to power, it focused on the nightlife at the seedy Kit Kat Club, and revolved around the 19-year-old English cabaret performer Sally Bowles and her relationship with the young American writer Cliff Bradshaw. A sub-plot involved the doomed romance between the German boarding house owner Fräulein Schneider and her Jewish suitor Herr Schultz. Overseeing the action was the Master of Ceremonies at the Kit Kat Club, serving as a constant metaphor of the tenuous, threatening state of the late period of Weimar Germany throughout the show.

Director: Omri Nitzan

Stage Designer: Roni Toren

Costume Designer: Orna Smorgonski

Lighting Designer: Avi Yona Bueno (Bambi)

Choreographer: Javier de Frutos

Video Editing: Ran Bogin

Video Designer: Shay Bonder

Photo Credit: Roni Toren

Due to its very particular background, reproducing Cabaret in Israel in 2011 had a special meaning, as a remembrance of the past and reflection on the present. In the production process, as the time background featuring the main "hero", the designers had taken inspiration widely from 1920's artists and artistic movements, such as Grosz and Otto Dix, and theater artists Piscator, Caspar Neher and Brecht, from Dadaism to Constructivism, as well as the period photography.

In this imaginative stage design, it showed 10 huge walls covered with blown-up newspaper clippings. Special printing techniques on wooden panels mounted on Aluminum frames formed sliding walls to create varied sceneries by projection mapping. An instrumental ensemble of sole women performers sat high on a moving platform, under which performed were well trained dancers. Through the whole piece, episodes of authentic documentary movies and pictures from that period were projected onto the sliding walls and screens behind the orchestra. The succinct stage was equipped with 22 chairs for interior scenes, and cabaret scenes, as a part of the choreography.

DON GIOVANNI, ISRAEL

• Radiant Color + Movable Diaphragms

This opera featured the travel of the main character Giovanni, who moved from place to place through, riding a motorcycle, flying a balloon, getting off a boat or train. He was destroyed at the end of the opera by his tormented enemy–women.

Director: Micah Lewensohn

Set Designer: Roni Toren

Costumes Designer: Buki Shiff

Lighting Designer: Avi-Yuna Bueno

This set won a silver medal at the W.S.D (World Stage Design), 2005 in Toronto. Red color was all over the stage, almost unbearable to watch, to resemble the obsessive, compulsive and excessive nature of the character, with the main concentration on the front diaphragm which moved in and out like an eye iris as the major setting.

Other characters all have their unique color of representations. Highly stylized visual images in primary colors: a line of blue ciders, a yellow fountain, a huge white moon etc., a mixture of sharpness, humor, naivety and cruelty added up to the dangerous and sarcastic atmosphere, to go along with the music in different episodes. Giovanni was finally devoured and nothing was left behind but his dressing gown. All were relieved, set was flown away, and the magic was gone just like the empty back stage.

על כל החרדות את חייבת לגבור.
Dispel your grief and fear.

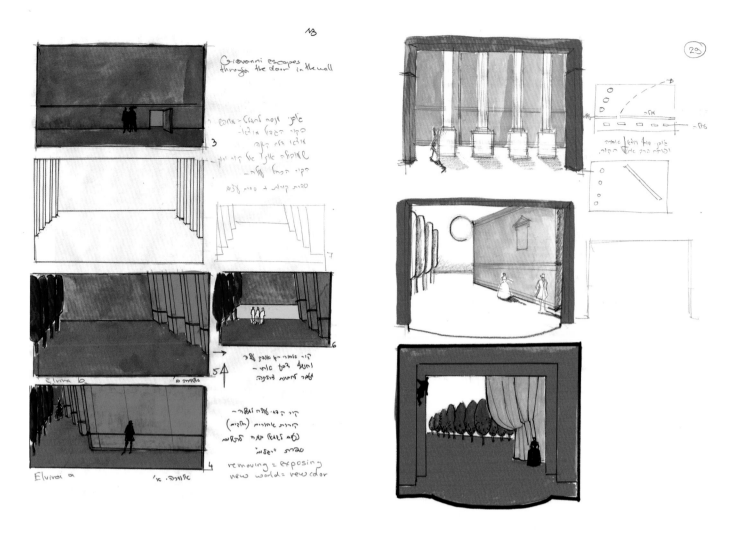

Giovanni escapes
through the door in the wall

removing = exposing
new world = new color

is thus the ungrateful man

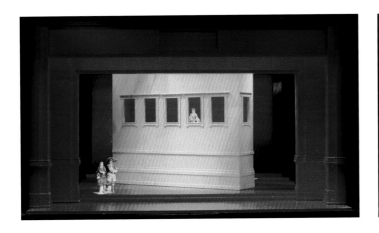

בורות בקומת קרקע – 1) סוגר את קצית מבמן להאטמא
אבסלוט כל שיה שמאל,
2) אם 30ים – את קצית מימן,
כל ירד אשר אם לש.

Harvey

• *Fluent Set Transition*

Harvey, the Pulitzer Prize–winning comedy by playwright Mary Chase, has returned to Broadway at Studio 54. Harvey is a story about a man with his imaginary friend, a pooka and his story with his sister. It is about the belief in the magic and goodwill that surround us all.

Design Company: Rockwell Group

Director: Scott Ellis

Set Designer: David Rockwell

Client: Roundabout Theatre Company

Photo Credit: Paul Warchol

The play was set in its original time–the 1940s, so as to infuse the entire design process with naturalism. All the way down to the wallpaper, brocade and backdrop-painting style, were loyal to the story.

The set and play consisted of two environments: the Sanitarium and the Dowd Family mansion. Quick and easy transitions between the two were made possible by dividing each setting into three sections. Seams between sections were disguised by the architecture of each location, allowing fluency of sets. With proper lighting, the transition can happen quickly and smoothly in the full view of the audience. Windows used were created by using light boxes. For the Sanitarium, the design is quite spa-like as it was in the nineteen-thirties/forties with an opulent hotel look. The Dowd Family Mansion went back to American Victorian period, capturing the grandeur of that time by stressing the library and the entrance hall designs.

iTMOi

• Simplicity + Impact

iTMOi is a reinvention of Stravinsky's ballet The Rite of Spring at its 100 anniversary by British choreographer Akram Khan, which is the acronym of "In the Mind of Igor". It also caused an uproar as the original work did and received wide-rangin criticisms for not only firstly changing the name of the ballet and but also not using any piece of music from Stravinsky.

Creative Director: Akram Khan

Stage Designer:: Matt Deely

Lighting Designer: Fabiana Piccioli

Costume Designer: Kimie Nakano

Photo credit: Jean-Louis Fernandez

"In this work, the designer is interested in the dynamics of how Stravinsky transformed the world of classical music by evoking emotions through patterns, rather than through expression, while these patterns were rooted in the concept of a woman dancing herself to death. This approach is a huge inspiration for me. But in a sense I hope to reinvestigate it, not just through patterns, as Stravinsky did, but also through exploring the human condition." – Akram Khan

The set consisted of a black dance floor, with shiny black square outlines, a floating shiny black frame and a golden sphere. Upstage was a gauze and BP screen for lighting. Through the show, the floating frame raised and tilted to various levels and at times emitted smoke, combined with lighting to carve geometric shadows on the floor as a floating symbolic element in the space. The gold sphere later flied in, swung and interacted with the performers.

Kinky Boots

• Scene Contrast + Lightening Design

Kinky Boots is a Broadway musical based on a 2005 British film of the same name. Set in a shoe factory, the story follows the main character as he attempts to save his family's shoe factory with the help of a vivacious drag queen, both of which find they have more in common than they've ever dreamed. What the story tries to convey is that by changing your mind about someone, you change your world.

Director: Jerry Mitchell

Design Company: Rockwell Group

Set Designer: David Rockwell

Musical Director: Cyndi Lauper

Photo Credit: Paul Warchol

The goal of this design was to create an environment that could transform over the course from one scene to another, collaged with peripheral scenes. It was inspired by utilitarian factories of the late 19th and early 20th centuries. For the scene in the factory, three curved iron trusses receding in the background were suspended above the stage. The walls were composed of fragmental iron work, brick and tinted glass windows. Racks of shoes, supplies, replicas of old equipment, LED lighting and four custom-designed working conveyor belts completed the purposely cluttered picture.

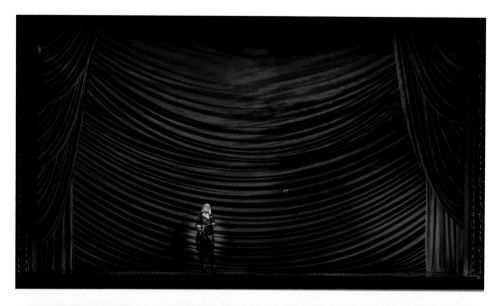

For the final runway scene in Milan, three drapery pieces flied in to cover the outside walls of the factory. Mirror panels randomly attached to sleek and black tubular steel walls gave life to the stage and lit up with color-changing LED fixtures that revealed multicolored shoe silhouettes. A flashing bubble light wall, composed of over 1,500 light bulbs on a mirrored surface helped to create a high fashion fun house that stood in stark contrast to the staid, iron and brick world of Price & Son shoe factory. Transformation of scenes had become possible by making the stage a two-tiered unit which could be rolled away with two mobile staircases.

Lucia di Lammermoor

• Mirror Floor + Tree Background

This work is by Italian composer Domenico Gaetano Maria Donizetti. The story concern the feud between two Scottish families, entwined with a tragic romance between two lovers, ending up with their death.

Staging Director: Catherine Malfitano

Scenic Designer: Wilson Chin

Lighting Designer: Duane Schuler

Costume Designer: Terese Wadden

Music: Gaetano Donizetti

Client: Lyric Opera of Chicago

The design team moved the time period of the tragic opera to the early 1800's when the book and opera were written, emphasizing the lush romance and dark, haunted atmosphere with a psychological edge. As critic John von Rhein at the Chicago Tribune commented, "Director Malfitano keeps the tale of illicit lovers moving swiftly, within uncluttered set designs by Wilson Chin that combines postmodern abstraction with period realism." The surrounding walls were based on the painted trees of David Caspar Friedrich, but distorted to look like a Rorschach test. Scenic designer Wilson Chin used a mirrored deck to reflect and double all the characters and give the impression of a world submerged in water. A large Wolf's Crag tower and a steep spiral staircase were set at the center of the stage, providing a claustrophobic playing area for the mad scene.

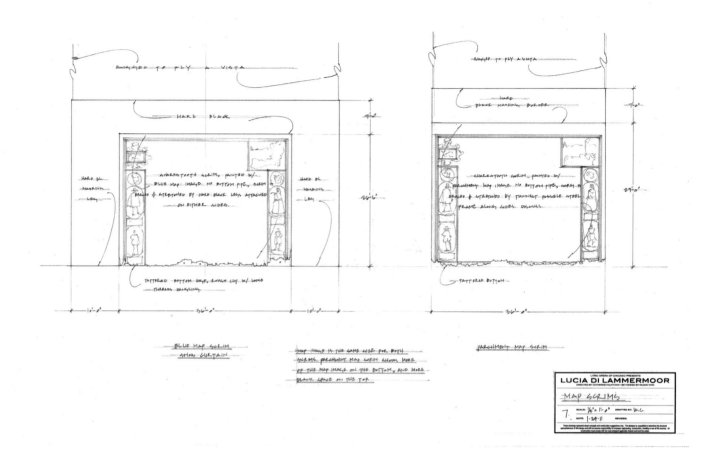

BLUE MAP SCRIM
SHOW CURTAIN

PARCHMENT MAP SCRIM

MAP IMAGE IS THE SAME SIZE FOR BOTH
SCRIMS. PARCHMENT MAP SCRIM SHOWS MORE
OF THE MAP IMAGE ON THE BOTTOM, AND MORE
BLANK SPACE ON THE TOP.

LYRIC OPERA OF CHICAGO PRESENTS
LUCIA DI LAMMERMOOR
DIRECTED BY CATHERINE MALFITANO · SET DESIGN BY WILSON CHIN

MAP SCRIMS

7.

SCALE: 1/4" = 1'-0"   DRAFTED BY: W.C.
DATE: 1·24·11   REVISED:

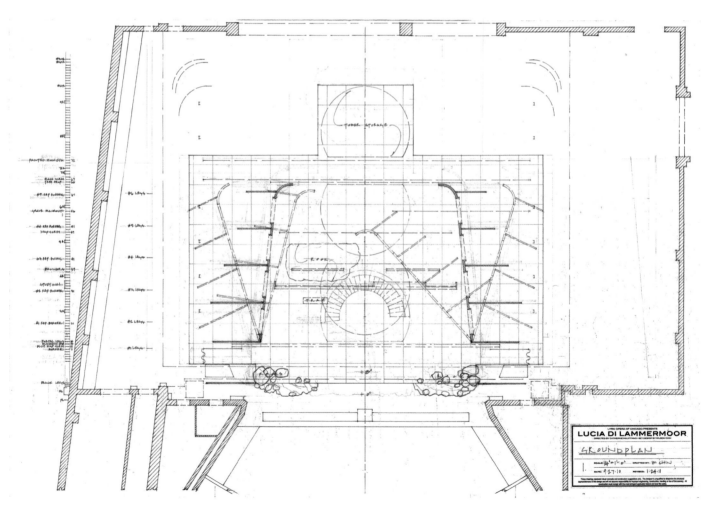

LYRIC OPERA OF CHICAGO PRESENTS
LUCIA DI LAMMERMOOR
DIRECTED BY CATHERINE MALFITANO · SET DESIGN BY WILSON CHIN

GROUNDPLAN

1.

SCALE: 1/4" = 1'-0"   DRAFTED BY: W. CHIN
DATE: 9·27·10   REVISED: 1·24·11

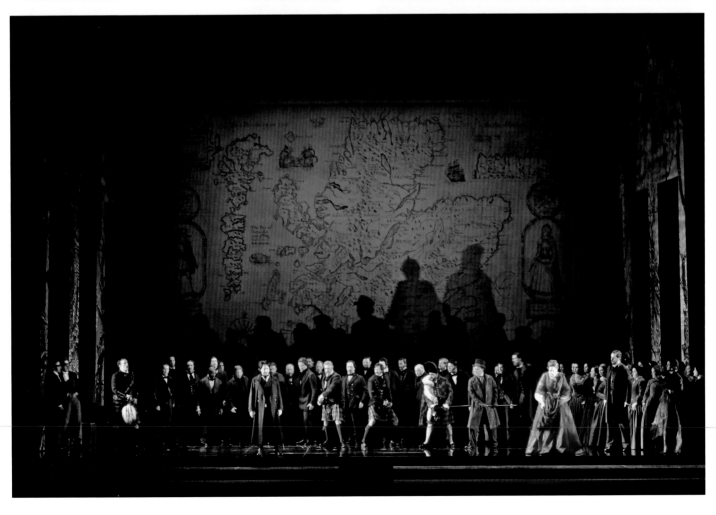

The Normal Heart

• Carved Walls + Projection Mapping

The set for this 1985-produced American play The Normal Heart featured names and a state-by-state death toll of the nation's AIDS victims. Rockwell Group's goal was to honor the spirit of the original production while simultaneously to craft an installation/performance space, as a memorial to the victims.

Director: Joel Grey, George C. Wolfe

Set Designer: David Rockwell

Photo Credit: Jeff Goldberg

The set was made up of three large white walls that contained 6,310 individually attached cut-out letters to form the sentences recounting early events of the AIDS crisis between 1980 and 1984, when the city failed to acknowledge the growing epidemic. To retain the emotion and rage in the script, play projections and light were reflected on the walls, which read like bricks or a textured surface. After intermission, they were replaced by a projection of names of people who have died in the crisis—in this way history becomes legible. This forms a literal, dramaturgical backdrop for Act II.

Felix Turner'a Desk at The New York Times

Scenes were given projected descriptions on a plain white header that floats, joined to ceiling joists above the stage. While the walls were plastered over with an off-white compound that helped to give it neutrality for all the settings. By accentuating the space with objects and furniture, Rockwell Group was able to specify a time and a place in the 80s' world.

Toward the end of the play as the leading character were frustrated and emotionally overwhelmed, the walls began to disappear, whereas there was just a vast blackness that encompassed the entire auditorium, linking the events of the play and the past to the audience and to the present.

Tartuffe

• *An Upside-down Cityscape Background*

Tartuffe is one of the most famous theatrical comedies by Molière, and the main characters of Tartuffe, Elmire, and Valère are considered among the greatest classical theatre roles. In contemporary French and English, the word "tartuffe" is used to designate a hypocrite who ostensibly and exaggeratedly feigns virtue, especially religious virtue. The play was written in 1,664 with the entire form of twelve-syllable lines (alexandrines) of rhyming couplets.

Scenic Designer: Wilson Chin

Lighting Designer: Matthew Richards

Costume Designer: Ilona Somogyi

Sound Designer: Fitz Patton

Client: Westport Country Playhouse

Wilson Chin set this comedy in contemporary France, but seen through the prism of Moliere's period. He fashioned an upside-down 17th century Paris cityscape on the wall of Orgon's house as the background, both a mural and a commentary on the topsy-turvy state of the household. At the end of the play, an extended paean was contributed to the glories of King Louis XIV, against whose reign the story was set. Chin used the black and white drawing of Paris and many doors in the background wonderfully.

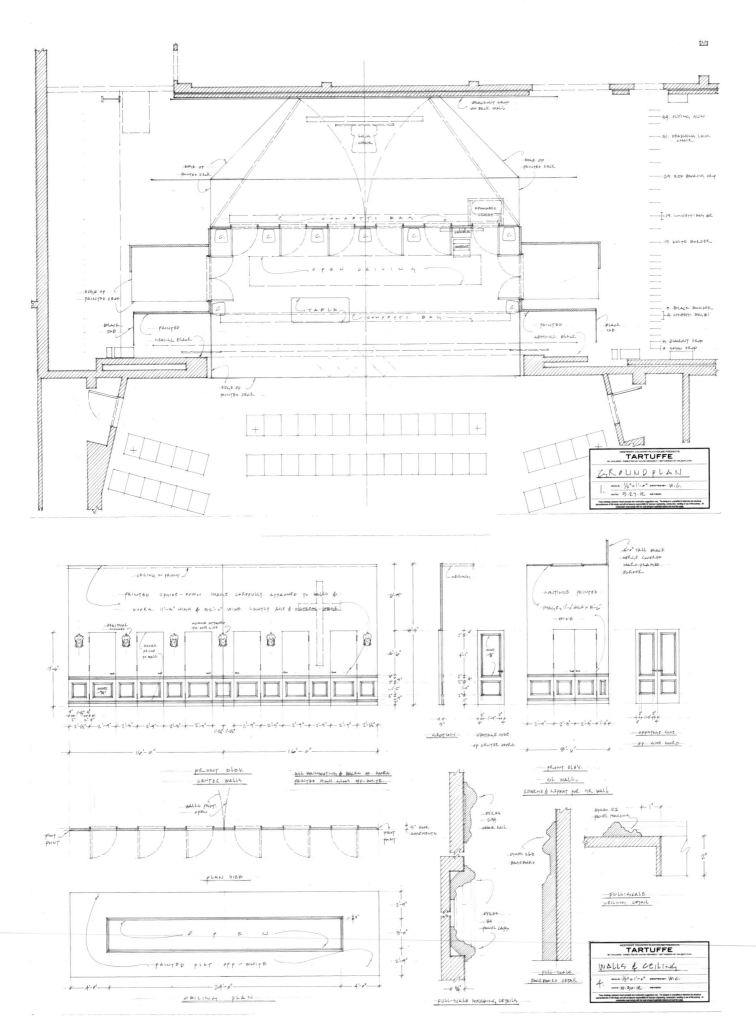

The Master and Margarita

• *Projection Mapping*

Mikhail Bulgakov's devastating satire of Soviet life—The Master and Margarita was written in secret during the darkest days of Stalin's reign. It contained two parts, one set in ancient Jerusalem, one in contemporary Moscow: the novel veered from moods of wild theatricality with violent storms, vampire attacks, and a Satanic ball, to such somber scenes as the meeting of Pilate and Yeshua, and the murder of Judas in the moonlit garden of Gethsemane, to the circus-like reality of Moscow. It was a world that blends fantasy with chilling realism, an artful collage of grotesqueries, dark comedy, and timeless ethical questions.

Director: Simon McBurney

Production Designer: Es Devlin

Costume Designer: Christine Cunningham

Lighting Designers: Paul Anderson

Video Designer: Finn Ross with additional animation

by Luke Halls for Treatment Studio

Visual Consultant: Willie Williams

As the team worked on The Master and Margarita, they read Bulgakov's letters together with the performers to build the sense the writer had formed: no one would leave Stalin's Moscow—all routes out were blocked. For the stage environment, the only way to penetrate the surface of the bricked up windows was developed by projection, thus by imagination. ES Devlin said, "when you see an image of a wall exactly projected on an identical 'real' wall, and when one wall starts to fall and the other remains standing, you hold onto two parallel realities."

In the Sign of Libra: A Wall of Wooden Closets

• A Wall of Wooden Boxes

The play based on stories by Croatian writer Ranko Marinković was crafted for stage by dramaturg Matko Botić and director Olja Lozica. The plot was about an old man's returned to his childhood island and encountered the same old humiliating situations he had long forgotten. Different aspects of humiliation were told by body language, rhythmic percussive sounds and invented gibberish words.

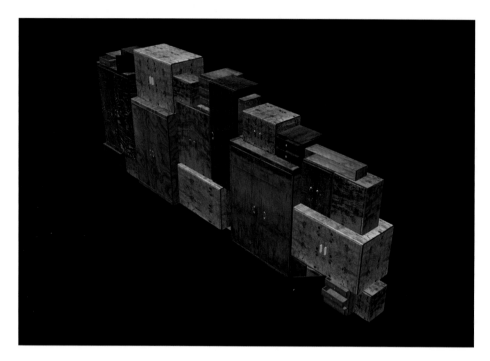

Director: Olja Lozica

Stage Designer: Igor Vasiljev

Costume Designer: Mario Leko

Lighting Designer: Deni Šesnić

Photo Credits: Igor Vasiljev

The main design element was a structure, a wall made of wooden cupboards and drawers. The central space was a box stuffed with books—that was the place the old man was located, surrounded by the characters and spaces of his imagination and memory, who had occupied various micro spaces within the cupboards and saturated with intimate histories.

The set included a tiny kitchen, a small bathroom, living room, study and sleeping room, each with a door to be stripped off the box and banged against the frame and the floor as an act of violent eruption. The floor was covered with reflective material which brought up the notion of water and, at an abstract level, of memories and imagination, in contrast with the two heaps of gravel on the front ground of the structure. At the turning point of the plot, traces of warm shines and the cyclorama slowly lighted up in the background. The structure receded into a silhouette. The audience and the protagonists were immersed in a sublime space of longing and waiting for the arrival of a ship.

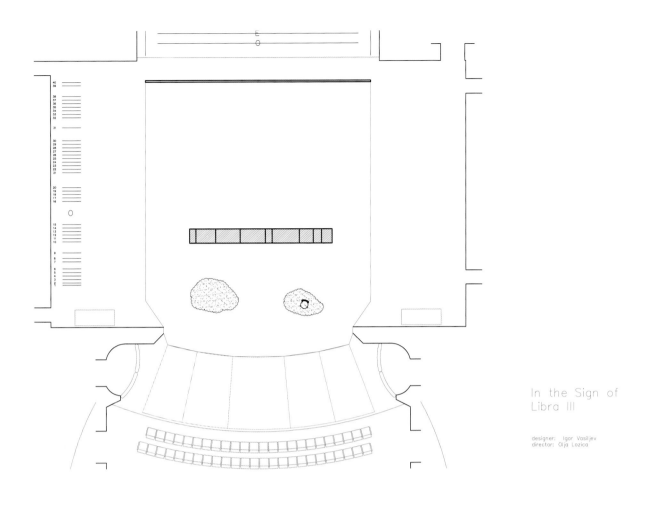

In the Sign of
Libra III

designer: Igor Vasiljev
director: Olja Lozica

Uncle Vanya

• *Layers Portals + Projection Mapping*

Uncle Vanya is a famous play by the Russian playwright Anton Chekhov. It surrounds the family members of an elderly professor, including his second wife, his daughter by his late first wife, his first wife's bother and his doctor friend. The present production was based on the rewritten English version by Irish playwright Brain Friel, keeping the original plot while adding a specia flavour of Irish-English idioms.

Director: Mick Gordon

Stage and Video Designer: Igor Vasiljev

Costume Designer: Maja Mirković

Lighting Designer: Mark Howland

Sound Designer: Mike Furness

Photo Credits: Igor Vasiljev

The design consists of a light box backdrop and four portals covered with printed images. The portals flied down from above the stage subsequently for each act, gradually overlapping each other. As for the furniture, there were nine white thonet chairs and a small table with a samovar. Printed images in the background were variations of the same motif, a mimic of birch forest. As the play evolved, the season progressed from summer to autumn, introducing a natural and even cosmic cycle. In this way, the characters were wrapped in a vast dimension of space and time to transcend and yet influence their limited actions and lives.

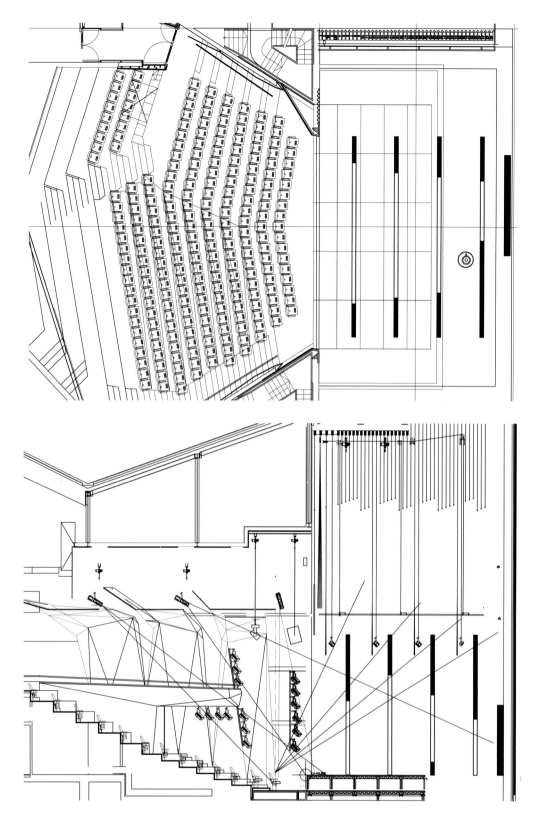

On the other hand, by introducing portals, the actual playing space becomes physically smaller and smaller, and the action taking in place became more intimate. Firstly, it started in front of the house in a public open space, then into the dining room, to the living room and finally bringing the audience into the main character's working room—the heart of the estate. At the end, leaves flying away from the tree branches with the sound of a light breeze was achieved by projection mapping over the printed surface.

Catch Me If You Can

• *Seamless White Backdrop*

After a successful run at Seattle's 5th Avenue Theater, "Catch Me If You Can" opened at the Neil Simon Theater on Broadway on April 10, 2011. Rockwell Group have transformed this tale of travel and deception for Broadway.

Design Company: Rockwell Group

Set Designer: David Rockwell

Client: Neil Simo Theater

Location: Broadway, USA

The musical did not unfold as a conventional narrative, but was told from the point of view of Frank Abagnale, Jr. himself. Rockwell Group therefore created a series of transient and ambiguous spaces to reflect the sensibility of the lead character. The set design was inspired by the beautiful and organic forms of airports and airplanes in the 1960s. Rockwell Group was also heavily influenced by popular looks from that era, including the seamless white backdrops behind TV Spectaculars, as well as the sharp, crisp, color-block graphics of movies, record covers, advertising and signage.

Medea & Edipo a Colono Scenography

• *Concave Blade*

Massimiliano and Doriana Fuksas has designed the facility for the Ancient Greece tragedy Medea and Edipo a Colono, scheduled at the Greek Theater in Siracusa.

Designer: Massimiliano Fuksas, Doriana Fuksas

Client: INDA Istituto Nazionale Dramma Antico

Photography: Moreno Maggi

Location: Siracusa, Italy

For the architects, the element of reflection and inspiration for the design of the set was the horizon. They designed a "concave blade" on the stage that reflected what was going around, which involved the public and invited reflection. The "concave blade" functioned as a mirror that also reflected the reconstruction of a lost horizon and the reality of the scene because reality is what we see in the mirror or what is reflected.

AIDA

• Floating Stage

The stage features a stunning floating platform and giant sculptures that bring the audience to the mystic scenes of the play, ensuring a magical experience for everyone present.

Stage Designer: Johannes Leiacker

Artist: Karl Forster

Verdi's Aida is one of the most popular operas of all time. This stage from the 2009 and 2010 summer Bregenz Festival brought a fresh look at this classic: the action took place on Bregenz's famous "floating stage", turning Austria's Lake Constance into the Nile River for the evening. Although this production was in many unconventional ways, the music and drama were actually intensified by the setting. The location enhanced the grand passion and tragic conflict of the story, with superb music. The Bregenz floating stage and Giuseppe Verdi were really a perfect combination.

✶✶✶
INDEX

✱✱✱

ACKNOWLEDGEMENTS

We would like to thank all the designers and contributers who have been involved in the production of this book. Their contribution is indispensable in the compilation of this book. We would also like to express our gratitude to all the producers for their invaluable opinions and assistance throughout this project. And to the many others whose names are not credited but have made specific input in this book, we thank you for your continuous support.

FUTURE COOPERATIONS: If you wish to participate in SendPoints' future projects and publications, please send your website or portfolio to editor01@sendpoints.cn